D0481317

PRAISE FOR *WHAT MADE JESUS MAD?*

"Are you ticked off at religion? So was Jesus. Are you sick of church-going finger-pointers? So was Jesus. Are you weary of people who call themselves God-fearers but behave like people-haters? So was Jesus. This insightful book invites us to explore the oft overlooked indignation of Christ. Be prepared to be convicted, instructed, and encouraged."

—MAX LUCADO, PASTOR AND
NEW YORK TIMES BESTSELLING AUTHOR

"Too many Christians have turned a blind eye to the stories and practices that actually made Jesus angry. In his book, *What Made Jesus Mad?*, Tim Harlow gives practical steps for living out a life that truly mirrors Jesus'. This book is an eye-opening take on present-day Christianity—specifically, what we are getting wrong about Jesus. If you are confused, frustrated, or plain angry about what you see happening around you, this is the book for you."

—CRAIG GROESCHEL, SENIOR PASTOR OF LIFE.CHURCH
AND *NEW YORK TIMES* BESTSELLING AUTHOR

"This book is refreshing, honest, and significant. Anger is a powerful emotion necessary to evoke change, ignite deep desire, and burn for justice in this world. No wonder Jesus got angry. If ever there was a time to explore the kind of anger that could help us confront evil, overthrow injustice, and right the things that are wrong on this earth, it is now. I believe Tim has put his finger on an important source of inspiration for this time. May the righteous anger of Jesus move us to actions that empower!"

—DANIELLE STRICKLAND, SPEAKER,
AUTHOR, AND SOCIAL JUSTICE ADVOCATE

"I had originally planned on speed-reading through *What Made Jesus Mad?* due to my hectic work schedule, but the book's title hooked me so much, and the content was so engaging, that I spent days neglecting work just to finish this thing! I really feel in my heart that this book is meant for the entire body of Christ—male and female, young and old, as well as all denominations."

—BRIAN "HEAD" WELCH, CO-FOUNDER OF THE BAND KORN,
NEW YORK TIMES BESTSELLING AUTHOR OF *SAVE ME FROM MYSELF*,
AND CO-STAR OF THE SHOWTIME MOVIE *LOUD KRAZY LOVE*

"As I began to read *What Made Jesus Mad?*, I didn't expect to see glimpses of myself in people who made Jesus mad. Scratch that—I was shocked to see much of myself in those who frustrated Jesus. Thankfully, Tim Harlow would rather help us love others well than scold us. Be prepared to put down the magnifying glass, look in the mirror, and love like Jesus, regardless of the critics."

—WILFREDO "CHOCO" DE JESÚS, AUTHOR AND
PASTOR OF NEW LIFE COVENANT IN CHICAGO

"Tim Harlow has hit the nail on the head. Too many Christians have turned a blind eye to the stories and practices that actually made Jesus angry at the church. Thankfully, Tim shows us what a true Christ-follower needs to look like in this book."

—MARK BATTERSON, LEAD PASTOR OF NATIONAL
COMMUNITY CHURCH AND *NEW YORK TIMES*
BESTSELLING AUTHOR OF *THE CIRCLE MAKER*

"Tim Harlow has written a book that asks the provocative question of what makes Jesus mad. The short answer is: us. At least, those of us who claim to follow him but so often get it wrong. The long answer is: you have to read the book, and then you will have a better chance of living in such a way that you bring a smile to many faces, including the Face that matters most."

—JOHN ORTBERG, AUTHOR AND PASTOR

"Only a man with a lifetime experience as a pastor could have the insight to write a book about challenging the people of God to reflect on what made Jesus angry. Tim Harlow is that man, and I recommend you read *What Made Jesus Mad?* and prepare to be challenged."

—ALAN ROBERTSON, AUTHOR AND PREACHER/DUCK HUNTER

"I have always wondered whether I would have been on the right side of history had I lived in Jesus' day. Would I have sided with Jesus or with the religious leaders who ended up killing Him when he showed up? Tim Harlow makes me feel even less comfortable asking that question, which is exactly why you should read this book. Tim holds nothing back in *What Made Jesus Mad?* He shines a light on the things that made Jesus angry and draws a parallel to our present-day church. Throughout the book, Tim gives practical steps for living out a life that truly mirrors Jesus'. Tim is an excellent guide for a journey that Christians and the church today need to take."

—CAREY NIEUWHOF, AUTHOR AND
FOUNDING PASTOR OF CONNEXUS CHURCH

"I love this book! Tim Harlow reveals the cringeworthy hypocrisy, legalism, and arrogance of the church—and why those of us who do our best to love like Jesus can so easily and unknowingly miss the mark. But Tim is a compassionate and humble insider who provides practical guardrails and biblical solutions for genuinely living out God's love. How? Surprisingly, by seeing exactly what made Jesus mad. This thought-provoking book is for everyone who is dedicated to following Christ's example of love, and everyone who is having a tough time following Jesus because they've seen too many Christ-followers do it poorly."

—LES PARROTT, PHD, PSYCHOLOGIST AND AUTHOR OF
LOVE LIKE THAT: 5 RELATIONSHIP SECRETS OF JESUS

"This is not a book about anger. It's a humor-filled, scripture-loaded, super-readable treatise about honesty, love, and the importance of being real before God. I highly recommend it to college students recovering from 'Zip Up Your Pants' church youth groups that only teach one lesson, and definitely to all churchgoers and anyone who wishes to know Jesus."

—SARAH SUMNER, PhD, AUTHOR OF *ANGRY LIKE JESUS:*
USING HIS EXAMPLE TO SPARK YOUR MORAL COURAGE

"Tim goes right at the heart of legalism in *What Made Jesus Mad?* and reminds us that our mission and mandate is to get people in, not to keep people out. Some of what's in the book might make *you* mad, but you should read it and ask, 'Do my life and values reflect the life and values of Jesus?'"

—ED STETZER, AUTHOR OF *CHRISTIANS IN THE AGE OF OUTRAGE*

"Some people might have trouble imagining an angry Jesus, but the Gospels are filled with evidence that Jesus came hard after anyone or anything that separated people from his Father. That means *What Made Jesus Mad?* isn't some fluffy reflection on a watered-down Savior. It's a twenty-first-century wake-up call that warns each of us to avoid repeating some dangerous first-century mistakes."

—DAVE RAMSEY, BESTSELLING AUTHOR AND
NATIONALLY SYNDICATED RADIO SHOW HOST

"Tim Harlow loves God deeply and loves people relentlessly. Regardless of your mistakes, who you voted for, and even if you're not a Bears fan—Tim is gonna love you. I've always wondered how he lives this way, but thankfully he's taught us how in *What Made Jesus Mad?* You'll learn what made Jesus mad, who He loves, and how you can live the same."

—CALEB KALTENBACH, FOUNDER OF THE MESSY GRACE GROUP
AND AUTHOR OF *MESSY GRACE* AND *GOD OF TOMORROW*

"Jesus was most definitely his Father's son. In his very own words, he reveals that he only does what he's seen his father do, and as joint heirs with Christ, we share the same spiritual DNA. If you've ever been frustrated, hurt, or even angry with ministry, Christians, or the church in general, take a number. Jesus was too. In this book, my friend Tim explores how, on many occasions, our New Testament Christ displayed that he inherited his Dad's Old Testament temperament. If you really want to know what made Jesus mad, don't let anything get in the way of you reading this book!"

—MONTELL JORDAN, PASTOR, AUTHOR,
MULTIPLATINUM RECORDING ARTIST

WHAT MADE JESUS MAD?

REDISCOVER THE BLUNT, SARCASTIC,
PASSIONATE SAVIOR OF THE BIBLE

TIM HARLOW

NELSON
BOOKS

An Imprint of Thomas Nelson

Published in Nashville, Tennessee, by Nelson Books, an imprint of Thomas Nelson. Nelson Books and Thomas Nelson are registered trademarks of HarperCollins Christian Publishing, Inc.

Thomas Nelson titles may be purchased in bulk for educational, business, fund-raising, or sales promotional use. For information, please e-mail SpecialMarkets@ThomasNelson.com.

Unless otherwise noted, Scripture quotations are taken from the Holy Bible, New International Version®, NIV®. Copyright © 1973, 1978, 1984, 2011 by Biblica, Inc.® Used by permission of Zondervan. All rights reserved worldwide. www.Zondervan.com. The "NIV" and "New International Version" are trademarks registered in the United States Patent and Trademark Office by Biblica, Inc.®

Scripture quotations marked CEV are from the Contemporary English Version. Copyright © 1991, 1992, 1995 by American Bible Society. Used by permission.

Scripture quotations marked ESV are from the ESV® Bible (The Holy Bible, English Standard Version®). Copyright © 2001 by Crossway, a publishing ministry of Good News Publishers. Used by permission. All rights reserved.

Scripture quotations marked KJV are from the King James Version. Public domain.

Scripture quotations marked THE MESSAGE are from The Message. Copyright © by Eugene H. Peterson 1993, 1994, 1995, 1996, 2000, 2001, 2002. Used by permission of NavPress. All rights reserved. Represented by Tyndale House Publishers, Inc.

Scripture quotations marked NASB are from New American Standard Bible®. Copyright © 1960, 1962, 1963, 1968, 1971, 1972, 1973, 1975, 1977, 1995 by The Lockman Foundation. Used by permission. (www.Lockman.org)

Scripture quotations marked NKJV are from the New King James Version®. © 1982 by Thomas Nelson. Used by permission. All rights reserved.

Scripture quotations marked NLT are from the Holy Bible, New Living Translation. © 1996, 2004, 2007, 2013, 2015 by Tyndale House Foundation. Used by permission of Tyndale House Publishers, Inc., Carol Stream, Illinois 60188. All rights reserved.

Any Internet addresses, phone numbers, or company or product information printed in this book are offered as a resource and are not intended in any way to be or to imply an endorsement by Thomas Nelson, nor does Thomas Nelson vouch for the existence, content, or services of these sites, phone numbers, companies, or products beyond the life of this book.

ISBN 978-1-4002-0860-9 (HC)
ISBN 978-1-4002-0861-6 (eBook)
ISBN 978-1-4002-1606-2 (ITPE)

Library of Congress Control Number: 2018964089

Printed in the United States of America
19 20 21 22 23 LSC 10 9 8 7 6 5 4 3 2 1

*For Charlie, Olivia, George, Caleb, and
the grandchildren still to come.
I dedicate this book to your generation, promising
to do my best to leave the church to you in a
way that would make Jesus happy.*

CONTENTS

FOREWORD

I'VE KNOWN TIM HARLOW FOR a long time, and one of the things I appreciate about him is that he is a man of both strong convictions and extraordinary grace. This combination makes him one of my favorite people when it comes to talking about Jesus. He can challenge a person who grew up in church their whole life to see Jesus in a new way, while in the same breath, compel someone who had never associated with church to examine the real Jesus. I'm not sure which category describes you. If the first, this book will challenge and maybe offend you. If the latter, this book will make you admire Jesus, even if you're not sure you want to.

I grew up learning about Jesus. But I wasn't introduced to the Jesus you'll get to know in this book. Instead, I was told about the flannelgraph Jesus. Flannelgraph Jesus is a favorite of the American church because he is soft and controllable. Flannelgraph Jesus doesn't get mad or say things that make you cringe. With flannelgraph Jesus, you can avoid those messy, uncomfortable Jesus stories that cause you to scratch your head and quickly skim over.

After hearing the same stories of flannelgraph Jesus again and again, I started to wonder: Is this the real Jesus? Was he just a nice person who gave gentle nudges in the right direction? Always giving hugs and only occasionally smacking your hand if you disobeyed? Because that is also how I would describe my grandma. But if Jesus was as sweet and congenial as my grandma, why were people so threatened by him that they killed him? When you start to set aside your preconceptions about a flannelgraph Jesus and begin to understand that he was a revolutionary, it changes the way you live as his follower.

Consider this book a garage sale of your religious ways. Maybe it is time for you to take an honest look at your life, and let go of certain traditions or passed down interpretations that don't accurately reflect the life of Jesus. Maybe it's time to slaughter some sacred cows, throw them on the grill, and have a party, because Jesus didn't call you to live a flannelgraph life. Each chapter in this book helps you work through some of the religion that has kept you and others at a distance from Jesus, but it is going to require some brutal honesty and some humble self-awareness on your part.

As you begin reading this book, stop for a moment and consider if you really want to know the real Jesus. Not just the Jesus who comforts, but the Jesus who confronts. Not just the Jesus who brings peace, but the Jesus who provokes. Not just the Jesus who teaches, but the Jesus who gets mad. If you're tired of living a carefully curated and comfortable version of Christianity, then I invite you to dig your hands into the messiness of the gospel.

The writer of Hebrews captures the essence of this book you're about to read: "And let us consider how we may spur one another on toward love and good deeds" (Heb. 10:24 NIV). The Greek word for spur means to provoke and irritate. It isn't a word typically used in a positive context, but in this passage, it is calling us, at the very least, to be willing to make each other uncomfortable so we could look more like Jesus.

There may be times when a phrase or a story in this book irritates you, or maybe even offends you, but I believe Tim's words about Jesus will spur you on to live a life that more accurately reflects the heart of Christ. If we want people to find and follow Jesus, then we have to be willing to remove the things that keep people from seeing him, even if it goes against our long-standing traditions. Hear me out. This doesn't mean watering down the message by any means, but it does mean accurately living it out and getting rid of what undermines it. After reading this book, I'm convinced that there is nothing more important than to make it our aim to be mad about the things Jesus was mad about, and to be for the things Jesus was for.

If that's truly the desire of your heart, then I believe you will love this book—even if you don't like it.

KYLE IDLEMAN
BESTSELLING AUTHOR OF
NOT A FAN AND *DON'T GIVE UP*

INTRODUCTION

Getting in the Way of God's Love

"If Jesus Ain't Happy . . ."

WE'VE GOT A MAGNET ON our kitchen refrigerator that says, "If *Momma* ain't happy . . . ain't *nobody* happy." It's funny, because we all know it's true. I want to make one for the church that says, "If *Jesus* ain't happy . . ."

We're so used to Jesus being portrayed in such a gentle and tenderhearted way that it can feel a little odd to think about him being unhappy with us, right? But I've spent a lot of time reading, preaching, and teaching the words of Jesus, and I believe the red-letter passages—those words spoken directly by Jesus—are quite appropriately, angrily red.

Let me say up front so you know where I stand: Jesus *was* nice and loving. He said things like "Love your enemies and pray for those who persecute you" (Matt. 5:44) and "Come to me, all you who are weary and burdened, and I will give you rest. Take my yoke upon you and learn from me, for I am gentle and humble in heart" (Matt. 11:28–29).

That sounds nice, right? But what about this? "You snakes! You brood of vipers! How will you escape being condemned to hell?" (Matt. 23:33). If someone tweeted that today, it would seem a bit inflammatory, don't you think? That was Jesus!

Though he was loving and tender, his words were sometimes sharp and biting. Many of the things Jesus said were either a direct condemnation of someone's attitude or behavior, or a story told to illustrate that condemnation.

We often learn more about a person from the things they *don't* like than what they *do* like. As a kid, did you ever do something that made your parents mad? Yeah? And the next time you thought about doing it, did you hesitate for just a minute? I remember calling my dad a name one time, and then . . . I never did it again. To this day, I can't tell you his favorite television show or his favorite breakfast cereal, but I know one name he does not like to be called. Note to self.

To be clear, anger is not wrong; it is *not* a sin. Paul said, "In your anger do not sin" (Eph. 4:26). Jesus' own brother, James, said we should be "slow to anger" (James 1:19 NASB), not *never* angry.

> We often learn more about a person from the things they *don't* like than what they *do* like.

Clearly, what we do with our anger can be wrong. Jesus spoke against that as well, telling us that we can murder with our hateful words (Matt. 5:22). Hatred, rage, and uncontrolled anger are terrible and sinful. But there is a godly kind of anger, one that causes you to want to do something *positive* about the *negative*. This is exactly what Jesus did with his anger.

If you know anything about Jesus' life, when you first read the title of this book, your mind likely went to the scene where Jesus threw the money changers and animals out of the temple. Exactly. Jesus was angry, and he did something positive with his anger. He didn't say, "What in the name of *me*!" and go Incredible Hulk on them. He channeled his zeal in positive ways. He *did* overturn tables and throw corrupt people out of the temple, because he was rightfully angry.

> So he made a whip out of cords, and drove all from the temple courts, both sheep and cattle; he scattered the coins of the money changers and overturned their tables. To those who sold doves he said, "Get these out of here! Stop turning my Father's house into a market!" (John 2:15–16)

He made a *whip*. He *drove* out. He *scattered*. He *overturned*. And he said, "How dare you!"

Other times Jesus threatened people with damnation. He used some seriously condemning imagery with the church leaders. He called people not-so-flattering names. He warned that it would be better if they had a big rock tied around their necks and were thrown into the sea (Matt. 18:6). It seems almost scandalous, doesn't it? But what if we're missing something by rushing past these uncomfortable displays of Jesus' passion and anger? What if, by unflinchingly digging into these passages of Scripture, we come to know a Savior who is so much more than we thought?

Here's an experiment for you: try reading only the red-lettered words of Jesus through the Gospels. You might be surprised by his frankness and emotion.

What Made Jesus Angry?

In every scriptural instance where Jesus expresses anger—the rawest of all emotions—this is the match that lit his fuse: *Do not get in the way of God's love.*

Think about it this way: Jesus came to provide his people direct access to the Father as demonstrated by the veil in the temple being torn at the crucifixion (Matt. 27:51). This was an enormously symbolic part of the crucifixion that most people miss. The area behind the veil was the Holy of Holies, where God dwelt. Only the high priest could go into the Holy of Holies, and only once a year. It was such a holy place that they literally tied a rope with a bell around the priest's leg to pull him out in case he had a heart attack when he came in contact with the Creator of the universe. If the bell stopped ringing, they started pulling.

No one else was allowed to go in, ever. God set it up this way because, although he wanted his people to know how much he wanted a direct relationship with them, there was too deep a divide between their sinfulness and his holiness. He was preparing them for a Savior.

At the crucifixion, the veil was torn "from top to bottom." This was God's way of showing us that Jesus' mission was complete.

> For God so loved the world that he gave his one and only Son, that whoever believes in him shall not perish but have eternal life. For God did not send his Son into the world to condemn the world, but to save the world through him. (John 3:16–17)

Everything Jesus came to accomplish had to do with reuniting the Father with his children. So if access to the Father was Jesus' purpose on earth, then it logically follows that it angered Jesus the most when people created barriers to that access.

There are three obvious instances of Jesus' anger in response to the barriers people put up:

1. In the temple, where money changers were literally denying access to the Father, especially for the non-Jews and the poor.
2. During his teaching, when little children were denied access.
3. On the Sabbath, when religious leaders put rules above relationship and suffering above healing.

There are many more times when Jesus' language seems to be directed in anger. I mean it's hard to call someone a "child of hell" (Matt. 23:15) with a smile on your face. Go ahead. Try it.

Did you notice at whom his anger was most often directed? It was at the religious people of his day. Well, the *leaders* of the religious people. That would be me today, okay? He was mad at the people who supposedly spoke for God. He was angry because they were blocking the little people from him: children, non-Jews, women, tax collectors, prostitutes, and sinners. Nope. Access denied.

It's very easy for the church today to fall into the same bad behavior that the Pharisees, Sadducees, and religious teachers exhibited in Jesus' day. But we have less excuse for blocking access to the love of the Father, because we're supposed to be learning from the example of Jesus! Which leads me to ponder what Jesus might think if he came to my church and observed the way we are helping people connect to the love of the Father—or denying them, as the case may be. Would Jesus like my church? Would he attend my church?

Believe me, I don't need that kind of pressure. But the question is thought-provoking, isn't it? If Jesus was angry with the church he encountered in biblical days, would ours fare better? They were following their interpretation of God's Word, just like we are. Granted, before Jesus came it had been 400 years since anyone had heard from God (Malachi), and the Old Testament did leave itself open to a great deal of confusion with all its rules and laws. But it's now been over 2,000 years since Jesus spoke, and I can't help but wonder how far the current church has drifted.

I want to be honest with you as we begin this journey together. James said, "Not many of you should become teachers . . . because you know that we who teach will be judged more strictly" (James 3:1). That verse makes me want to retire, or at least throw up. So allow me to let you off the hook right here. I'm writing this book to myself, and to the past two thousand years of church leaders who have missed the point. Most of us have good hearts, but many of us are exactly like those to whom the angry red letters were directed.

What Made Jesus Cringe?

What was it that made Jesus cringe? Religious phonies, arrogant judges, unjust legalists, and hypocrites. They make me cringe also! Right up until the time I examine myself and realize that my own natural gravitational pull veers in the same direction. The real tragedy about this propensity we all have to drift from God's heart is what it does to those who may have been led to believe that Jesus doesn't want them around, or that Jesus is to blame for the legalism, judgment, and hypocrisy of the church, when nothing could be further from the truth. All Jesus ever wanted was for them, for me, for all of us, to come home.

In the movie *Gladiator*, the central character, Maximus, states, "Caesar once had a vision of what was supposed to be Rome, and this is not it."[1] Like Maximus, I believe Jesus had a vision of what the church was supposed to be, and many times, where we have ended up is not it.

My friend Caleb's parents split up when he was very young, and he grew up living with his mom and her lesbian partner. When he got older, he became a Jesus-follower, but with a different perspective because of what life was like for him growing up. I've known Caleb for years. We both share the same heart for Jesus and those far from him. We have talked at great lengths about how the actions, bitterness, and even hatred of some Christians have driven people further away from Jesus. Caleb has preached at my church and I've done interviews with him, but I was particularly moved by one story he told me that illustrated this phenomenon:

> Some Christians are still shocked when I tell them that I marched in pride parades with my mom and her partner, Vera. It never fails. There's usually someone who immediately asks if I saw anything inappropriate during the parades. I tell them that I remember marching in one parade when I was nine years old and seeing inappropriate things . . . but probably not the inappropriate acts they're referring to.
>
> When we first arrived for the parade, I remember noticing how kind the other parade participants were. They asked me how old I was, what I wanted to be when I grew up, and even offered me water during the march. The floats, clothing,

and signs were all very colorful. The brightness of the colors matched the celebratory attitudes of those in the parade. There was also music, laughing, dancing, and it seemed like a really fun party.

As the parade went on, more and more people began lining up on the sidewalks to support the parade. At some point, someone gave me a sign to carry that compared fundamentalist pastors to Nazis. I felt important, because when I held up the sign, people on the sidewalks would clap and cheer me on.

While there were a few people doing sexual motions on some of the floats, the most inappropriate thing I saw that day was at the end of the parade. There were supposed Christians holding up signs that said things like, "God hates fags" and "No room for you." If that weren't offensive enough, when people from the parade walked over to dialogue with them, they were sprayed with water and urine.

Those being sprayed yelled back at the angry Christians, "Why are you treating us like this?!"

I was horrified. I asked my mom and Vera why Christians would act this way. My mom looked at me and said something to the effect of, "Caleb, they're Christians, and Christians hate gay people. If you're not like them, they will not like you."

So when asked if I saw anything inappropriate during the parades, I'd say, "Absolutely. The reaction of the Christians at the end of the parade was so inappropriate that it made me despise all Christians and assume that Jesus must be horrible if his followers were this awful."[2]

Is it true that Christians hate gay people? Christians aren't supposed to hate anyone. Jesus told us hate is the same thing as murder (Matt. 5:21–22). So it should be easy to answer. There is no planet in existence where spraying urine on someone can be reconciled as loving your neighbor as yourself (Matt. 22:39). This is a radical example, but we all know many just like it.

Throughout history, many have tried to pull the kingdom back to the vision of Jesus. Charles Dickens took a shot in *A Christmas Carol*. Scrooge is complaining to the second spirit about the things done in "his" (God's supernatural kingdom) name. The spirit is more than a bit put off and replies, "There are some upon this earth of yours who lay claim to know us, and who do their deeds of passion, pride, ill-will, hatred, envy, bigotry, and selfishness in our name, who are as strange to us. . . . Remember that, and charge their doings on themselves, not us."[3]

Ouch. How easy it is for us to get away from the heart of how things were meant to be. We, who claim to know Jesus and do things in his name, must seem very strange to him. The incredible irony is that we oftentimes exhibit the exact same actions and motives that caused a spike in Jesus' blood pressure back in his day. We, who claim to know his Father today, are also getting it wrong. The world around us doesn't have a problem with Jesus. Most of the time it's his followers they have a problem with.

David Kinnaman of the Barna Group did a research project with the goal of assessing self-identified Christians to determine if their attitudes and actions toward other people are more like Jesus or the Pharisees. He said, "our intent was to create some new discussion about the intangible aspects of following and representing Jesus." They tried to identify qualities of Jesus, such as empathy, love, and faith—or the "resistance to such ideals in the form of self-focused hypocrisy."

Curious? He found that 51 percent of Christians identified

themselves more strongly on the Pharisee side, while only 14 percent (one out of seven) seemed to represent the actions and attitudes consistent with Jesus, as identified by the Barna Group.[4]

There's a bumper sticker that sarcastically cries, "Lord, save us from your followers." Think about this. Jesus could have had the same sticker: "YHWH, save me from your followers." It wouldn't have mattered, though. God's followers ended up killing him.

Yes, these were God's church members yelling, "Crucify him!" Church members who were swayed by their church leaders to reject Jesus and his silly idea of God's love for everyone. Jesus knew it was going to happen, and he even asked God to forgive them while he was hanging on the cross. But sometimes their attitudes must have made him crazy mad.

Thankfully, when Jesus rose again, many of these same people rejected their church's rejection of him, went back to following him, and found the truth. Luke tells us that Christianity spread like crazy (Acts 2:47), even under the threat of extreme persecution. Because once they finally understood the principle of having access to God and living in grace, people loved it.

What I'm saying is, if you or one of your friends are having a hard time following Jesus and being in a relationship with your Father in heaven because his followers have been badly representing him, there is still hope for things to be different.

Access Granted

One of my good friends became a paraplegic in an accident when he was nineteen. For over twenty years, he's been my partner in building a church that helps people find a relationship with their heavenly Father. Lonnie is amazing. It's hard to understand what it's really like for someone who is unable to use their legs until you get close to them. There were so many things I didn't realize.

When Lonnie first joined us, he drove a regular car with hand controls. But to get in, he had to wheel up to the passenger side, swing himself into the seat, take his wheelchair apart and put it in the back seat, and then slide over to the driver's side. He did that multiple times a day. Now he has a van, but it's still not as easy as it looks. In fact, it wasn't until we traveled and stayed in a hotel together that I got a clear picture of what he has to go through just to do the everyday things we take for granted.

They say you never really understand a person until you walk in their shoes. Walking with Lonnie—or rolling with Lonnie in his wheelchair—has changed my perspective and makes me grateful for the many handicap parking spaces in front of the stores. I'm all for the Americans with Disabilities Act that requires public places to be made accessible to all. And that's what we want spiritually as well.

If you're reading this book and you're confused or upset because the church dumped on you or you've been hurt by one of its many hypocrites—stay with me. Jesus wants you to know that is not the way he wants it to be.

If you are a Christian trying to walk faithfully but struggling to see how to do so, let's look with fresh eyes at the attitudes that made Jesus angry and see if we can move things in the right direction. If we could learn, or relearn, the heart of Jesus, we could play a more effective role in accomplishing his goal.

So, wherever you are coming from, let's dig into Scripture together and get to know the Savior who was blunt, sometimes sarcastic, and wildly passionate about giving people access to the Father.

CHAPTER 1

WHEN INSIDERS GET IN THE WAY

Throwing Tables

On reaching Jerusalem, Jesus entered the temple courts and began driving out those who were buying and selling there. He overturned the tables of the money changers and the benches of those selling doves, and would not allow anyone to carry merchandise through the temple courts. And as he taught them, he said, "Is it not written: 'My house will be called a house of prayer for all nations'? But you have made it 'a den of robbers.'"

The chief priests and the teachers of the law heard this and began looking for a way to kill him, for they feared him, because the whole crowd was amazed at his teaching.

(Mark 11:15–18)

THE LOGICAL PLACE TO START a study on the anger of Jesus would be the "opening up a can of . . ." incident, as I call it, in the temple when he overturned the tables and threw

1

out the money changers. How can we not start there? Also, this most famous expression of Jesus' anger precisely illustrates the point of denied access. But we may need to dig in a little deeper than what you've likely been taught in the past.

There are many ways to interpret anything, especially when something was written for a different culture by people from a different place and period in history. We are always looking through personal lenses we may or may not even realize are there. For example, Paul explicitly commanded the church in one of his letters to "greet one another with a holy kiss" (Rom. 16:16). It was in the imperative tense, in the Dad voice, a command. It was evidently an important part of that culture. In some cultures, kiss greeting is still in practice, but I don't know a church in the United States that is obeying Paul's command. Nobody is smooching in my lobby, and I probably have more Italians at my church than you do. Why aren't we kissing?

This concept isn't easy, and it's not the point of this book. But we need to think it through before we can really understand Jesus' anger. Let me explain some categories of bad Bible interpretation. I'll call the first category Gummy Bears interpretation, which is applying what you want while ignoring what you don't want. Our church used to have an office next to a candy store. It was the nineties, and all the nutrition talk was about fat content. So I tried to watch my fat intake as I walked into the candy store. I know. I know. Just let me tell you how I justified it. I got a bag of gummy bears because they are fat-free! Never mind that they are basically just melted globs of sugar and high-fructose corn syrup. I didn't want to hear about that! In my mind, it was all fine as long as it was fat-free. Much of our bad

Bible interpretation follows the same logic when we pick and choose the things we like and ignore what we don't.

Why did we decide, for instance, that it was okay to go *against* 1 Timothy 2:9 and allow women to wear jewelry, but *obey* 1 Timothy 2:12 and not allow women to teach men in some congregations? Those are four verses apart! How do we reconcile 1 Corinthians 11:5, which talks about women prophesying in public, against the "command" for women to be silent in church in 1 Corinthians 14:34–35?

The question of tattoos fits here also, even though forbidding tattoos is part of the old covenant, which we'll talk about in a second. Why do so many Christians believe tattoos are wrong? The injunction against tattoos (Lev. 19:28) was in the same biblical chapter that rules against shaving (v. 27) or wearing clothes made of two different kinds of fabric (v. 19). Somehow many—maybe most—Christians still think tattoos are bad, yet a poly-cotton-blend shirt is acceptable. Gummy Bears: ignoring one thing while emphasizing another.

Let's call the second category the Sister-in-Law interpretation, which is applying rules that are no longer binding. Deuteronomy 25:5 tells us that if a married man dies without a son, his widow "must marry her late husband's brother" (CEV). Sounds like a good plot for a reality television show, but I don't see that working today.

The problem with this interpretation arises when we take the rules from the Old Testament and try to make them apply to our lives in the post-law, New Testament era. The issue is that these are rules we're no longer obligated to keep (Col. 2:14; Gal. 3:13). Trust me when I tell you that you don't want to head down the path of trying to follow the Mosaic law. I'll give you one reason: bacon (Lev. 11:7–8).

The third category I'll call the Bake Sale interpretation. These are the rules we create based on a completely incorrect interpretation of a specific passage of Scripture, even under the new covenant. For example, in some churches, bake sales are not allowed in the building because everyone knows we "don't sell stuff in church." The reason is obvious, right? Because Jesus threw the money changers out of the temple. But was that the point Jesus was making? Was he mad about selling things in general? Was it that they were overcharging? Or was it much deeper than that?

Let's go back and take a closer look at the Mark 11 passage about Jesus' anger in the temple, which I would submit has nothing to do with selling stuff in church. How do we know this? Let's break this down, starting with verse 17: "Is it not written: 'My house will be called a house of prayer for all nations'? But you have made it 'a den of robbers.'" There are three parts to this statement:

1. house of prayer,
2. for all nations, and
3. den of robbers.

Let's take a closer look at each one.

House of Prayer

By the time Jesus was born, it was standard practice to sell the animals used in the temple sacrifice. It was more convenient for travelers who no longer had to bring the animals to the temple.

The service of the money changers also made things easier for travelers who had to pay the temple tax with a certain type of currency. It was more efficient to both exchange the money and buy the sacrifice once they got to the temple. If you modernize the concept to online church giving, it will make more sense. You can bring your offering envelope or your check (if you still have a checkbook), but I find it more convenient to do it online.

So, was Jesus' anger mainly because they were doing all this in the house of prayer? I definitely think so, but can we rid the world of one terrible interpretation of this story?

Acts 17:24 tells us, "The God who made the world and everything in it is the Lord of heaven and earth and does not live in temples built by human hands." We don't worship in a temple anymore, because in the post-Jesus era the temple is gone. God's house is not the church building! The church building is not the temple. To God, this is likely the most offensive part of this entire misinterpretation. In the old system, God knew that he needed a place to meet with his children, or, more correctly, a place where they could come to meet with him. While they lived as nomads in the desert, he had them construct a movable temple called a tabernacle. Then once they settled in the promised land, King David did a fund-raiser, and his son Solomon built the elaborate temple in Jerusalem. This is the temple building where Jesus started throwing stuff around.

The temple had different places where certain segments of the population were allowed to worship. The outermost area was the Court of the Gentiles, which meant that anyone could go there and worship. Next was the court for Jewish women, then the place for Jewish men. Yes, it was discriminatory; I won't argue with that. It was the old covenant, and God set it up how he wanted it and knew how the Jewish culture would accept it. But then Jesus came, and everything changed. Don't you just love Jesus even more for that?

Inside the Jewish boys' club was the Court of the Priests, where the religious leaders worshiped and offered sacrifices brought by the people. Beyond that was the innermost area, the Holy of Holies, where God's presence dwelt. It wasn't that God was limited to this spot; it simply represented a connection to his presence in a tangible way. However, as already mentioned, the presence of God was separated from everyone else by a thick veil.

The gospel writers record that the veil was torn from top to bottom (Matt. 27:51; Mark 15:38; Luke 23:45). This was not an accident; it was symbolic. Because of Jesus' sacrifice, there is now no separation between God and his people. There is no need for priests to sacrifice something for our sins. The perfect sacrifice was made once and for all. There is no need even for a temple; the temple is now in our hearts: "Don't you know that you yourselves are God's temple and that God's Spirit dwells in your midst?" (1 Cor. 3:16).

All of us now have an all-access pass to hang out with God any time we want. This is the essence of the gospel: access to God. We get to go backstage. Have you ever had a backstage pass? I will never forget the time I had the opportunity to officiate a wedding for a member of Styx. I love classic rock music, so I was thrilled. Yes, I know. Styx is the name of a river in hell. But the band was so good.

I had dinner backstage with the band that night and then sat in killer seats for their concert. We had a cue song so I would know when to go backstage and get ready. When the song "Mr. Roboto" came on, I grabbed my Bible and went to the door. I got in without question because I had the all-access pass, which, by the way, is still in my desk drawer in case the band gets back together. After their final song, the lead vocalist, Dennis DeYoung, came out and said, "Now we're going to have a wedding." He then introduced me to the crowd of 14,000 people, who were pretty wasted by this time. Right as I pronounced the drummer John Panozzo and his sweet fiancée, Jan, husband and wife, the guitarist Tommy Shaw started singing, "Oh, Mama, I'm in fear for my life from the long arm of the law . . ." It still gives me goose bumps to this day.

> All of us now have an all-access pass to hang out with God any time we want. This is the essence of the gospel. . . . We get to go backstage.

Oh yeah, the point is I had the all-access pass. That's what Jesus died to provide for you, which is why there is no need for a physical temple anymore. So to make a correlation between a modern church building and the temple is complete heresy. A church building today is just a place where people gather to worship. I'm not saying we shouldn't have respect for a building that was likely built on the sacrifices of some very godly people. I'm saying it's not the same as a temple; that is, it's not the dwelling place of God. This is my emancipation proclamation: I hereby pronounce emancipation for your church building from any rules that were meant for the temple. There are no theological conditions forbidding selling in the church or, more importantly, bringing coffee into the service. Can I get an "amen"?

In Jesus' day, however, the temple was still the house of prayer and the place where people had access to God, which is why Jesus was mad. We will come back to that later.

Den of Robbers and All Nations

Now that we've addressed the "turning the house of prayer into a market" problem, the next obvious issue is the robbery. The money changers charged a fee for the exchange, which was perhaps exorbitant, although we don't really have evidence of this from history. Another possibility is that inside racketeering was going on, with the church leaders receiving kickbacks on approved animals. For now, let's just place this in the same category as paying nine dollars for a Coke at a baseball game. You get the idea. You can complain about the "den of robbers" all day, but if you get thirsty at a baseball game, you don't have much choice. Sure, Jesus was unhappy with the price charged and the location chosen, but I don't believe that alone was the reason Jesus got angry.

Jesus was mad because of what always made him mad: denied access to his Father. Jesus was angry because of what was happening as a result of the money changers and dove sellers turning the "house of prayer" "for all nations" into a "den of robbers." My belief is that it was not one but likely a combination of all three parts of this statement that elicited Jesus' zeal. In keeping with what we know about Jesus, permit me to make a case for the less obvious "all nations" part.

Jesus was in the *outer* court, the "all nations" part of the temple, when he decided enough was enough. This was the Court of the Gentiles, far from even the area where the Jewish women gathered. It was the place where God provided access to the rest of the world. And this was where the "robbers" had set up shop.

Jesus' anger was directed at the Jews who turned the non-Jews' house of prayer into a market, thereby denying access, literally, to the outsiders who wanted to worship God. Making this area into a marketplace was not particularly conducive to worship either. In other words, the outsiders, those who felt furthest from the Father, were the ones who suffered the most. They were being robbed not only of their hard-earned money, by the exorbitant prices of the animals and exchange fees, but of their very access to God.

This was something Jesus cared deeply about. His anger was not just a split-second moment of passion. There is an important detail to this story that shows Jesus did not just fly off the handle in the temple that day. This event happened on the Monday morning of Jesus' final week before his death. The previous day, Jesus rode into Jerusalem as the crowds waved palm branches, believing he was coming to become the new king. Then on Palm Sunday night, he went into the temple: "Jesus entered Jerusalem and went into the temple courts. He looked around at everything, but since it was already late, he went out to Bethany with the Twelve" (Mark 11:11).

He knew what was going on already before the events that happened on Monday morning. So this isn't him just blowing his fuse suddenly. This was more than a hasty, in-the-moment statement about selling baked goods or T-shirts in the foyer. This was a thought-out, slow-burning conviction about the access God wanted people to have to him. John, who wrote his gospel many years after the other gospels, tells us that the disciples remembered this incident (John 2:17) as a fulfillment of an Old Testament prophecy: "Zeal for your house consumes me" (Ps. 69:9).

Does it make more sense now? Jesus wasn't zealous for the sanctity of the temple. He prophesied that it would soon be destroyed, and it was. Jesus was zealous for the access to God the temple provided. He came to rip the veil and give us an all-access pass to a beautiful relationship with our heavenly Father. The relationship for which we were created. He'll throw tables or animals or people out of the way to give us this all-access pass. He gave up his own life to get us backstage.

God wants us in. He's calling us in. And Jesus is never going to just stand by and let anyone or anything keep even one of us out. I apologize on behalf of the church if someone has done that to you or your friends. It was not and never has been Jesus' intent. As a matter of fact, he would create a scene in a holy place to make sure everyone has access. Especially the ones who are the furthest away.

CHAPTER 2

WHEN BEING GOOD GETS IN THE WAY

Hellboys and Hellgirls

"Woe to you, teachers of the law and Pharisees, you hypocrites! You shut the door of the kingdom of heaven in people's faces. You yourselves do not enter, nor will you let those enter who are trying to.

"Woe to you, teachers of the law and Pharisees, you hypocrites! You travel over land and sea to win a single convert, and when you have succeeded, you make them twice as much a child of hell as you are."

(MATT. 23:13–15)

LET ME TAKE YOU BACK to school for a moment. In any given classroom, you will always find three distinct groups of students. There are those who clamor for seats in the front row, those who do the same for the back row, and those I call the *hakuna-matata* students because they just walk in and sit wherever.

The polarity exists most distinctly between the front and the back. These groups of students have completely different approaches to school. The front-row kids like to sit there because they did their homework, and when the teacher asks a question, they can stick up their hands and say, "Oh, oh, oh, pick me!" These are the classmates who have the gall to remind the teacher if he or she forgets to assign homework for the evening. I don't know if their issues are genetic or learned, but it is a problem for the rest of the class. The back-row kids just want to have fun and get decent grades. Their propensity to sit in the back is mostly about distance from the teacher; the farther you are, the better your chances of getting away with things. As opposed to the temple system mentioned in the previous chapter, this is a matter of choice. These are my people. I love learning, but I also want to multitask while I'm at it. I may be the only person in history to receive a doctoral-level education entirely from the back row, while also playing video games. Can you say ADHD?

Some people love rules, and some don't. You probably aren't old enough to remember that people were allowed to smoke on an airplane. Although it seems ludicrous today to think that you can avoid secondhand smoke inside a pressurized metal tube, when airlines first introduced the ban to promote public health, not everyone was in favor of this new rule. Why do you think the flight attendants still have to announce that "smoking in the lavatories is prohibited by law"? Who doesn't already know that?

Most of us are happy for the rules and want to follow them. But some of us, even if we understand and believe in the rules, just don't *want* to.

Jesus Sat in the Back Row

In the beginning, God made civilization, by which I mean he gave his people a system of laws. Part of the definition of *civilization* obviously includes "civility." God instructed human beings on the basics of civility to establish order, which is wholly necessary, even for people like me who struggle with rules. You realize the importance of civil order when you become a parent. If you bring children into the family, you'd better be prepared to teach them some semblance of civility. If you don't have children, just go to Chuck E. Cheese's, and you'll understand.

Through the years, God's children tried to follow his system of laws. They mostly failed to do so, but there was at least a uniform standard in place. Because, you know, without a uniform standard, everything falls apart. Fast-forward to the transition of our calendar from BC to AD, and we find that the distance between the front row and the back row had grown very deep in Judaism. The people in the front row of religion were called the Pharisees, the Sadducees, and the teachers of the law. They followed rules as a way of life. As a matter of fact, they liked rules so much that they added their own rules on top of God's rules so they'd have more things to do right.

I believe they initially had good intentions, but by the time Jesus arrived, they had exponentially added more rules to the 613 commandments in the Torah. As if 613 weren't enough already. The result was that it became even harder to live in right relationship with God, which left the back-row folks—let's call them "sinners"—falling further and further behind. It was as if the front-row kids made the classroom larger and longer. At this point, if you were in the back row, the teacher was too far away, and you had little hope of even understanding the material, let alone applying it and getting a good grade. Then came Jesus, the long-awaited Messiah.

He was different from what anyone expected. You would have thought he'd sit in the front row and be the teacher's pet. But no. Jesus didn't sit in the front row very often. He didn't even spend much time in the middle. When Jesus went to class, he usually sat in the back row. Not because he wanted to play video games, but because he wanted to provide access to God for the ones who were furthest away.

> While Jesus was having dinner at Matthew's house, many tax collectors and sinners came and ate with him and his disciples. When the Pharisees saw this, they asked his disciples, "Why does your teacher eat with tax collectors and sinners?"
>
> On hearing this, Jesus said, "It is not the healthy who need a doctor, but the sick. But go and learn what this means: 'I desire mercy, not sacrifice.' For I have not come to call the righteous, but sinners." (Matt. 9:10–13)

Here's my paraphrase of Jesus' words: "I have come for the people in the back row, and I choose to sit in the back row with them." Jesus sat in the back, and when the teachers called on him, he went to the front of the class and gave amazing answers. Then he turned around and told the people in the front row that they had bad attitudes and called them hypocrites. With an exclamation point!

> "You hypocrites! Isaiah was right when he prophesied about you:
>
>> "'These people honor me with their lips,
>> but their hearts are far from me.

They worship me in vain;

their teachings are merely human rules.'"

(Matt. 15:7–9)

Sounds like Jesus was mad, doesn't it? He told them that even though they were naturals at religion and knew all the answers, they still weren't good enough to get into the kingdom. He said they needed to stop looking down on the people in the back row.

"How can you say to your brother, 'Let me take the speck out of your eye,' when all the time there is a plank in your own eye? You hypocrite, first take the plank out of your own eye, and then you will see clearly to remove the speck from your brother's eye." (Matt. 7:4–5)

Oh yeah, and he called them hypocrites again, just for good measure.

"Woe to you, teachers of the law and Pharisees, you hypocrites! You travel over land and sea to win a single convert, and when you have succeeded, you make them twice as much a child of hell as you are." (Matt. 23:15)

If that statement doesn't knock you back, you aren't reading it correctly.

Jesus was saying that the front-row system of rule-following is not of heaven; it's from hell. Not that following the rules is wrong. The problem is that the religious elite were making incorrect assumptions about what following the rules did for them. They assumed they could win God's favor if they were just good enough, and that God graded on a curve, meaning they were "in" regardless because everyone else was so below them (therefore "out"); in other words, they were in no matter what. Which, of course, is ludicrous. To even think that we, as fallen human beings, can somehow earn our way to the banquet table of God is absurd.

> When Jesus went to class, he usually sat in the back row. Not because he wanted to play video games, but because he wanted to provide access to God for the ones who were furthest away.

The apostle Paul said, "Therefore no one will be declared righteous in God's sight by the works of the law; rather, through the law we become conscious of our sin" (Rom. 3:20).

Maybe it's not just ludicrous; it's hellacious.

Children of Hell

The Pharisees were "children of hell" because they rejected God's provision for their salvation and attempted to justify themselves through their own righteous works. But the bigger problem was that these hellboys, with their "human rules" church system, were blocking the door to the kingdom of heaven for the people who were in the back of the classroom.

When religious leaders, like myself, give even the slightest hint that God loves his children more because they are being "good," we are literally playing into the greatest tactic hell has ever produced. It leads to pride among those in the front of the class, and despair in the back.

> Then some Pharisees and teachers of the law came to Jesus from Jerusalem and asked, "Why do your disciples break the tradition of the elders? They don't wash their hands before they eat!"
>
> Jesus replied, "And why do you break the command of God for the sake of your tradition? For God said, 'Honor your father and your mother' and 'Anyone who curses his father or mother is to be put to death.' But you say that if anyone declares that what might have been used to help their father or mother is 'devoted to God,' they are not to 'honor their father or mother' with it. Thus you nullify the word of God for the sake of your tradition. You hypocrites! Isaiah was right when he prophesied about you:
>
>> "'These people honor me with their lips,
>>
>>> but their hearts are far from me.
>>
>> They worship me in vain;
>>
>>> their teachings are merely human rules.'"
>
> (MATT. 15:1–9)

Let me point out that these church leaders came from Jerusalem. This means they were not only sitting in the front row, but they were on the highest honor roll. Jerusalem was the Ivy League. Jesus and his posse were in Gennesaret at the time of this story, so it appears that these leaders came on a mission to confront Jesus and chose to do so through the handwashing tradition his followers had ignored. This handwashing rule,

Yadayim,[1] was not one of the original laws God had given but had been added later by Judaizers.

There is, of course, nothing wrong with handwashing. The issue here was about the *way* they did their handwashing. The church leaders in Matthew 15 were offended because the disciples didn't do it in the annoyingly specific way according to a rule they had made up. This is the disconnect. I believe Jesus was purposefully pushing the church leaders' buttons. This handwashing thing was just another way in which Jesus was making a statement about the hypocrisy of "rules taught by men" and the problem it caused for people having access to God.

Instead of answering their accusations, Jesus launched a counterattack. He answered them,

> "And why do you break the command of God for the sake of your tradition? For God said, 'Honor your father and mother,' and, 'Anyone who curses their father or mother is to be put to death.' But you say that if anyone declares that what might have been used to help their father or mother is 'devoted to God,' they are not to 'honor their father or mother' with it. Thus you nullify the word of God for the sake of your tradition." (Matt. 15:3–6)

Instead of addressing their issue of handwashing, Jesus simply asked why they put tradition ahead of actual Scripture. In perfect Jesus fashion, he took it up a notch. He answered their question with a deeper question. Essentially, he said, "No, my followers didn't wash their hands the way you think they should, but let's talk about some things that are much more serious in relation to God's standards of civility. Let's skip from

Yadayim to Corban [another rule they had added]." You're going to love this!

Pharisees could declare a material possession Corban, which meant "devoted to God." It was just a made-up rule that basically meant, "I want to be selfish and do what I want with what I have and not worry about anyone else, even my parents." A good example of calling something Corban is like when we call shotgun for the front passenger seat in a car. According to Michael Scott, a character on the television show *The Office*, "The rules of shotgun are very simple and very clear. The first person to shout 'shotgun' when you're within sight of the car gets the front seat. That's how the game's played. There are no exceptions for someone with a concussion."[2]

Truthfully, this Corban concept was much worse than calling shotgun and forcing your concussed friend to ride in the back on the way to the hospital. This was about taking care of your own family. If you wanted to be selfish and not help support your own aging parents, you just needed to call Corban and "dedicate" your stuff to God (while you still used it). Doing so meant freezing your assets or money and leaving someone else to deal with taking care of your parents.

The brilliance of Jesus' example was that while the Pharisees were complaining about his disciples breaking the tradition of handwashing that had no basis in Scripture or had real bearing on anything of importance, such as ceremonial handwashing, they were clearly denying the teaching of the actual Word of God about caring for one's family, something that was extremely important.

I'm talking about the method they used to wash their hands versus one of the ten actual commandments given to Moses from God: "Honor your father and mother." It was on the tablet when Moses carried the tablets down the mountain, likely with dirty hands.

The Spirit of the Law

This breaking of the handwashing rule may have just been accidental in this instance, but we know that Jesus purposefully broke some of the religious leaders' other rules, or allowed his disciples to break the rules, to demonstrate that following the rules was not—nor had it ever been—the point.

Jesus addressed the real source of uncleanness, which is the *heart* of the matter:

> Jesus called the crowd to him and said, "Listen and understand. What goes into someone's mouth does not defile them, but what comes out of their mouth, that is what defiles them." (Matt. 15:10–11)

The Pharisees were missing the spirit of the law and the real reason for washing. If your ceremonial handwashing is a way to demonstrate your worship of God, then by all means go ahead and wash your hands. But if you think you're getting a better grade because you did it, then you have lost your way. In other words, if the way you raise your hands in worship or the posture you take in prayer helps you feel closer to God, that's fantastic. But don't look down on anyone else because they don't do it or do it differently.

More importantly, if you want to skip past a grace-filled

relationship with God, choosing instead a works-based striving to please a harsh heavenly Father, that's your business. It's frankly, child-of-hell business, but that's up to you. However, when you throw that attitude onto others, Jesus is going to get mad.

In the phrase "child of hell" (Matt. 23:15), Jesus used the term for "hell" to refer not just to an eternity away from God, but also to extreme punishment. In other words, as bad as this sounds already, it's actually worse. Jesus was saying they were deserving of extreme punishment, as well as an eternity away from God, because they were blocking the way for people to get to God by emphasizing their own rules over God's heart.

So much of what made Jesus angry—what Jesus taught and rebutted against the self-graded honor roll inductees in the Gospels—came from a need to refute these children of hell. He needed to refute them so they wouldn't keep teaching their students to "worship [God] in vain" (Matt. 15:9), creating double-hell kids.

We all probably need to spend more time in the back row, where a guy like me, like you, and like Homer Simpson, might be comfortable.

CHAPTER 3

WHEN RULES GET IN THE WAY

Homer Simpson Was Right

*And He [Jesus] entered the synagogue again, and a man
was there who had a withered hand. So they watched
Him closely, whether He would heal him on the Sabbath,
so that they might accuse Him. And He said to the man
who had the withered hand, "Step forward." Then He
said to them, "Is it lawful on the Sabbath to do good or to
do evil, to save life or to kill?" But they kept silent. And
when He had looked around at them with anger, being
grieved by the hardness of their hearts, He said to the
man, "Stretch out your hand." And he stretched it out,
and his hand was restored as whole as the other. Then
the Pharisees went out and immediately plotted with the
Herodians against Him, how they might destroy Him.*

(MARK 3:1–6 NKJV)

"'They worship me in vain;
   their teachings are merely human rules.'"

(MATT. 15:9; JESUS QUOTING ISA. 29:13)

TO ME, HOMER SIMPSON SUMMARIZED the issue of made-up rules. When he was asked what religion he belonged to, he said, "You know, the one with all the well-meaning rules that don't work in real life—uh, Christianity."[1] But is that really Christianity? Or has Jesus been misrepresented?

I believe Homer's statement accurately represents the world's view of Christianity. The irony and importance of this discussion is that it actually represents the same misconception that made Jesus angry with his church. Well-meaning rules that don't work in real life create a huge barrier.

I'm not a rule guy, as I've already established. My childhood was in the sixties and seventies. It's not that I question order or its purpose; it's the stupid rules that bug me. If you make a stupid rule, I will break it. Sorry, Mom.

Rumor has it that John Mellencamp wrote a song about me. "When I fight authority . . . [come on, you know it] . . . authority always wins." I'm the problem. I know. I'm a classic 8 on the enneagram scale.

This side of me made my life even more difficult when I decided to attend a very conservative Bible college, which had a lot of rules. One of their well-meaning rules that didn't work in real life was about facial hair. When at age eighteen I finally had some facial hair starting to grow, I had to shave it! So, for my first speech in freshman speech class, my topic was "Jesus Had a Beard."

Yes, I chose to begin my public speaking career by opposing authority in the institution where I would spend the next four years. That's me. I was incensed by the disconnect between the facial hair rule and the fact that Jesus did not have a razor and so likely looked like a hippie, and therefore would not have been admitted into this college that bore his name. Of course, Jesus didn't wear pants either, but I wasn't going to argue everything.

I'm older now, and I'm fairly certain this was not a new revelation to any of the faculty at the time. The school's point was that they believed it was a bad representation in the culture of our day, which was their right. They did change the policy eventually, and everyone looks like Jesus now. But I'm sure my speech had no impact.

Anyway, despite the rule, I stopped shaving during the last week of school in 1983 so I could have some rebellion stubble at graduation. I haven't had a clean face ever since. Funny thing is, I don't really like having a beard. I hate maintaining it and having it catch the drip of olive oil and parmesan cheese every time I eat Italian food. But subconsciously I believe I will never be able to shave my face for fear that I will be perceived as giving in to "the man." I heard an unsubstantiated story from way back in the school's history that women were not even allowed to wear polka-dot clothing because it might encourage the boys to want to—wait for it—poke the dots. I can't make this stuff up!

As much as I found—and still find—some of these rules ridiculous, I also realize that we, especially I, need guardrails. Society needs governance, and there is no way to govern without well-meaning rules. God gave us real rules because he loves us; each commandment was given for our benefit. Every good father knows he needs to teach his kids not to lie or steal. It never leads to a good place. What about adultery and murder? What would it mean for society if those rules didn't exist? Even the first five of the Ten Commandments, which are about our relationship with God, are for our benefit.

You can interpret the command "Thou shalt have no other gods before me" (Ex. 20:3 KJV) as a possessive or arrogant statement if you want. But I hear it like a dad talking to his children. As a dad, my commands are for my children's safety and best interests. When they were little, I told my children not to follow other dads.

Plus, many of God's real laws were about cleanliness and health, which benefits everyone. I mean, wash your hands, please. We know why that's important. There's even a sign about it in the gas station bathroom. God likes clean. He wants the best for us. He's our Dad.

I'll give you an example. In Deuteronomy, God instructed the Israelites to bury human waste products (I like the King James Version on this one; it smells better):

> Thou shalt have a place also without the camp, whither thou shalt go forth abroad.
>
> And thou shalt have a paddle . . . and it shall be, when thou wilt ease thyself abroad, thou shalt dig therewith, and shalt turn back and cover that which cometh from thee. (Deut. 23:12–13 KJV)

You see, people in those times didn't understand germs. They didn't "bury that which cometh from them." During the Middle Ages, Europe was nearly wiped out because they failed to heed this advice on cleanliness. As a direct result of dumping human waste into the streets, millions of people died from the Black Plague, a disease caused by the microscopic organism that thrived in human waste and was carried into the homes by fleas on the backs of rats!

I apologize if you are reading this near mealtime, but the truth is, God has always watched out for his children. Scholars estimate that one-third of the 613 regulations in the first five books of the Old Testament were included mainly for health reasons. Germs weren't discovered for thousands of years, but God (the Father) warned his children not to touch dead animals, not to use cracked pottery, to use running water to wash, and so forth, because he knew the germs were there.[2] Dad was taking care of us.

So, as much as I naturally want to rebel against ridiculous rules, please don't think I'm James Dean-ing here as I talk about the problem of legalism. Truthfully, I'm a rebel *with* a cause. And it's a very big cause for me.

The Dark Side of Christianity

The Simpsons is the longest-running television show in human history. The writers obviously understand our culture. In the show, the problem with Christianity lies with the character Ned Flanders, the uber-Christian. If you're not familiar with *The Simpsons*, Ned does live by Christian principles, but he's a little over the top about it. His doorbell plays "A Mighty Fortress Is Our God." He has a "Hallelujah Chorus" air horn for ball games. At Christmastime he answers his phone, "Christ is born. Who's on my horn?" And he takes baths in a swimsuit so as not to subject himself to his own nakedness.

These are the insufferable sides of Ned. But there are darker sides as well, like when he passed out pamphlets titled "You Will Die in Hell" at an outdoor movie. No wonder Homer has a bad taste for Christianity. But Ned doesn't represent who Jesus is. And he's not who Jesus wants us to be either, because it causes barriers for people like Homer. If Christianity seems odd to Homer, it's because Jesus has been badly interpreted by people like Ned. Homer hasn't had the chance to get to know the real Jesus.

Andy Stanley, senior pastor of North Point Community Church, gives this illustration:

> For a long time in my life, my approach to Christianity was kind of like a *Simon Says* game. Except it was *Jesus Says*. It kind of went like this:
>
> Jesus says, "Stand up."
> Jesus says, "Read your Bible."
> Jesus says, "Pray."
> "Sit down."
> Ah, Jesus didn't say to sit. Look over there. You're out.
>
> What I learned as a kid about this *Jesus Says* game is that it was very difficult to stay in the game, and then you'd get out and feel really guilty. The problem for me was, I got out a lot when I was young. I learned to sort of like getting out. If you got out, then you didn't have to play anymore. It was a very difficult game to play, because who could do everything Jesus says?
>
> I would get out, and I'd think, *Well, I'm out, because I blew it and I messed up and I sinned, so I think before I get back in the game, I'll just spend a few weeks sinning because I'm already out anyway. You know, it doesn't really matter!*[3]

Can you relate to Andy? The problem is that some people, like Ned Flanders, might be excellent at game playing, but not everyone is.

The greater problem, as Andy continues, is that:

Every once in a while, I'd meet people who had never played *Jesus Says*. They were, like, sinners and bad people, and I'd think, *You know, they really need to play* Jesus Says. But they don't want to. And a part of me envied them. They don't carry any guilt. They just kind of do whatever they want.

But then somebody would come along and say, "Andy, you need to go talk to all the people who don't believe in *Jesus Says* and tell them they need to play."

Which kind of makes sense, because Jesus is awesome. But I was never sure I wanted to tell them.[4]

It seems to me that a lot of people, like Homer Simpson—and maybe you—only understand Christianity as a game of *Jesus Says*. And what's incredible is that this is exactly the same situation Jesus was in with his church 2,000 years ago. If Homer Simpson were to have a conversation about "rules that don't make sense in real life" with Jesus, I could hear Jesus replying with, "Oh yeah? Let me tell you about Judaism. Let me tell you about the *God Says* game the religious elite tried to get me to play. And, by the way, they didn't just knock me out of the game; they had me executed because they couldn't handle the way I played."

Watch how Jesus played their *God Says* game one holy day:

One Sabbath, when Jesus went to eat in the house of a promi-nent Pharisee, he was being carefully watched. There in front of him was a man suffering from abnormal swelling of his body. Jesus asked the Pharisees and experts in the law, "Is it lawful to heal on the Sabbath or not?" (Luke 14:1–3)

Well played, Jesus! Ask the umpires for a ruling *before* you make the move. You see, the law said not to work on Saturday, but the Mishnah had to be consulted too. Mishnah was the addition and clarification to the law added by the Pharisees, which gave thirty-nine separate categories for the meaning of *work*. For example, the ruling was that you could spit on a rock on the Sabbath, but you couldn't spit in the dirt because then you'd be making mud. Seriously!

How did the Pharisees respond to Jesus' preemptive question?

> But they remained silent. So taking hold of the man, he healed him and sent him on his way. Then he asked them, "If one of you has a child or an ox that falls into a well on the Sabbath day, will you not immediately pull it out?" And they had nothing to say. (Luke 14:4–6)

In several passages where Jesus healed on the Sabbath, the Bible records that the Pharisees went outside and plotted how they could kill Jesus: "For this reason the Jews persecuted Jesus, and sought to kill Him, because He had done these things on the Sabbath" (John 5:16 NKJV). You have to love these rules. You can't heal on the Sabbath, but you can plot a murder. Okily dokily, as Ned Flanders would say.

Jesus decided it was time these Pharisees learned a lesson about forcing others to follow their perhaps well-meaning but don't-work-in-real-life rules, so he broke one of them. Cue the Mellencamp: "When I fight authority. . ."

Good People Doing Bad Things

British comedian Ricky Gervais says that "good people do good things, bad people do bad things, and when you find good people doing really bad things, religion is usually involved."

If someone knows Ricky, tell him I think he's hilarious, that my son-in-law is British, and I'd like to hang out. I get where he's coming from. Sometimes bad people do good things in the name of religion also. Ricky, I feel your pain. I think Jesus would too. I don't want to belabor the point, but it's pretty important: religion was involved in the execution of Jesus. So it's safe to assume Jesus was angry with religionists: "[He] looked around at them with anger, being grieved by the hardness of their hearts" (Mark 3:5 NKJV)—in other words, mad.

> You have to love these rules. You can't heal on the Sabbath, but you can plot a murder.

This must have made an impression on the disciples. The gospel writers tell us that they did not record everything Jesus did because there wouldn't have been room (John 21:25), but they *did* record seven different healing miracles on the Sabbath:

1. Cast an unclean spirit out of a man (Mark 1:21–28; Luke 4:31–37)
2. Healed Peter's mother-in-law from fever (Matt. 8:14–15; Mark 1:29–31; Luke 4:38–39)

3. Healed a man with a withered hand (Matt. 12:9–13; Mark 3:1–6; Luke 6:6–11)
4. Healed a lame man by the pool of Bethesda (John 5:1–18)
5. Healed a crippled woman (Luke 13:10–17)
6. Healed a man with dropsy (Luke 14:1–6)
7. Healed a man born blind (John 9:1–7, 14)

These were important miracles in their own right, but the gospel accounts seem to be less centered on the miracles themselves than on their rule-breaking nature, especially that they were Sabbath-breaking miracles. Jesus was more interested in doing good than following rules. A good Father would find his children's needs more important than a list of approved activities on a certain day. If you had a sick child, wouldn't you find a doctor who was open on the weekend/Sabbath?

Here's another example of Jesus breaking the Sabbath rule, and this time he was teaching in a church:

> Now [Jesus] was teaching in one of the synagogues on the Sabbath. And behold, there was a woman who had a spirit of infirmity eighteen years, and was bent over and could in no way raise herself up. But when Jesus saw her, He called her to Him and said to her, "Woman, you are loosed from your infirmity." And He laid His hands on her, and immediately she was made straight, and glorified God.
>
> But the ruler of the synagogue answered with indignation, because Jesus had healed on the Sabbath; and he said to the crowd, "There are six days on which men ought to work; therefore, come and be healed on them, and not on the Sabbath day." (Luke 13:10–14 NKJV)

Hang on. Let me switch to the King James Version for Jesus' response:

> Thou hypocrite, doth not each one of you on the sabbath loose his ox or his ass from the stall, and lead him away to watering?
>
> And ought not this woman, being a daughter of Abraham, whom Satan hath bound, lo, these eighteen years, be loosed from this bond on the sabbath day? (Luke 13:15–16 KJV)

Jesus essentially said, "You care more about your ass than you do this poor woman!"

Luke 13 tells us, "And when He said these things, all His adversaries were put to shame; and all the multitude rejoiced for all the glorious things that were done by Him" (Luke 13:17 NKJV). The gamers were shamed, and the people rejoiced.

I sure hope Homer Simpson can meet Jesus. At the very least, I want him to understand that Ned Flanders and Jesus aren't the same. Jesus didn't come to follow or break well-meaning rules; he came to fulfill them (Matt. 5:17–20). This is what Christianity is supposed to be about, not about well-meaning rules that don't work.

But humanity's default is to turn the relationship with our heavenly Father into a game. We just can't get comfortable getting the win for free because it feels like cheating, which of course it is; that's the essence of the gospel, the good news. Jesus told the man next to him on the cross, a man seconds away from the end of his execution for criminal behavior and had no way to get back in the game, "You win. I won the game for you."

Legalism Default

The sad irony is that the same disciples who rejoiced when Jesus put the rule-makers to shame went right back to legalism when they were left in charge.

The post-Jesus church leaders wrestled greatly as they tried to figure out the new rules. Namely, how to separate following Jesus from Judaism. As Jesus was the fulfillment of Judaism, it was much easier to figure out how to live in the grace of Jesus within the structure of Judaism. You either believed Jesus was the Messiah, or you didn't. But the game rules were still the same.

Everything was working well until the Gentiles came along, which was a game changer. Literally. They were forced to throw out the old game altogether. Actually, if I can change metaphors, it was more than a game changer—it was a change of the operating system. As I was working on this book, I thought of purchasing a voice-recognition software to make it easier for me to write. One particular software was better designed for Microsoft Windows than for Macintosh, which is what I've been using for ten-plus years. The sales guy kept trying to get me to switch my operating system so I could use his product. Um, no. I've hit Ctrl-Alt-Del for the last time.

Adding Gentiles to Christianity was like completely changing the operating system. These non-Jews wanted to follow Jesus, but they didn't feel the need to do it within the guidelines of Judaism. Okay, let's just be honest, there was one major issue involved: they didn't want to get circumcised.

If you were born into Judaism, you got the snip when you were eight days old. But if you wanted to convert to Judaism as an adult, well, this sacrament becomes a legitimate aversion to your faith. So the big argument in the beginning of the church centered around how Christians should observe the law. Could they eat meat sacrificed to idols? Should they still celebrate certain holy days? Were they obligated to marry their sister-in-law if their brother died without a son? And so on. It was all a part of the big discussion of Jesus versus the Old Testament laws. And circumcision was front and center in that discussion.

The apostle Paul got pretty fired up about it, especially in his letter to the church in Galatia. He emphatically stated, "For in Christ Jesus neither circumcision nor uncircumcision has any value. *The only thing that counts is faith expressing itself through love*" (Gal. 5:6, emphasis added). It sounds exactly like what Jesus did when he broke the rules and expressed love on the Sabbath, right? What if Homer Simpson could grab hold of that idea?

This isn't a book about Paul's anger, but he seems to take cue from Jesus' playbook and takes a pretty low blow at the legalists who were still trying to play religious games in the early church: "As for those agitators, I wish they would go the whole way and emasculate themselves!" (Gal. 5:12). Yep, he just said that. Can you imagine Paul's media team's reaction when he tweeted that one?

Here's the deal. The fallback position is always about rules. They make us feel safe. I was fascinated by this quote from Abraham Lincoln 1,800 years after Paul penned his acerbic words:

> I have never united myself to any church, because I have found difficulty in giving my assent, without mental reservation, to the long, complicated statements of Christian doctrine which

characterize their Articles of Belief and Confessions of Faith. When any church will inscribe over its altar, as its sole qualification for membership, the Savior's condensed statement of the substance of both Law and Gospel, "Thou shalt love the Lord thy God with all thy heart, and with all thy soul, and with all thy mind, and thy neighbor as thyself," that church will I join with all my heart and all my soul.[5]

Legalism puts up barriers to the Father. I'm sorry, Abraham. I'm sorry, Homer. I'm sorry, any of you readers who ever had Jesus misrepresented to you throughout your lifetime, especially if it was by me.

For the twenty-first-century church, legalism happens slowly over time, as it did for the religious system of Jesus' day. I love the story of the lady who always cuts the ends off her ham before she cooked it. When someone asked her why she did it, she said it was just what her mother always did. Perplexed, she later called her mom, who said she didn't know either; it was just what she'd been taught. They then got on the phone with Grandma and asked her, and she replied, solving the mystery, "It was the only way it would fit in my pan."

By the way, this Sabbath thing never really went away, even though the early church decided to worship on Sunday instead of on Saturday (Sabbath) because it was the day Jesus rose from the dead. The Jewish Christians could decide for themselves whether to still observe their Saturday Sabbath rituals, but Sunday became the corporate celebration time. Then, as time progressed, Christians made Sunday into a well-meaning rule with yet another Sister-in-Law interpretation (no longer binding). For example, pastors like me would often go so far as to reference this old command about the Sabbath to guilt people into coming to church. I've done it, and I apologize.

Not so long ago, towns were basically shut down on Sundays because it was "the Lord's day." I'm not saying this is a bad idea. I, for one, am grateful that Hobby Lobby closes on Sundays. It's part of their commitment to God and their workers' families (and it also gives my wife one less day to shop there). It's just that it was when Christians made the Sunday shutdown into a rule, it became one of Homer Simpson's "well-meaning rules that don't work," because some people have no choice but to work on Sundays. In fact, the early church likely met on Sunday night because their members had to work. Truthfully, the Sunday-morning-service-at-eleven tradition morphed around the farming community to give farmers time to milk the cows first. But it slowly transitioned from Grandma having a small ham pan into something we take as law.

One of my good friends grew up in a denomination that forbade certain activities on Sundays. It was a rule. Basically, the rule translated into, "God wants you to be bored on Sundays." They had a swimming pool but couldn't swim on a Sunday, for example; that is, until one fateful warm day when they invited the new pastor over for lunch after church. He saw the pool and asked, "Why don't we swim?" My friend said, "From then on, the pool was open 24/7, and God seemed . . . nicer."

Clearly, as a pastor of a church, I would argue that gathering for worship is important, and we should worship together. The writer of Hebrews told us not to give up meeting together (Heb. 10:25). I believe the church is the body of Christ, and it's hard for the body to work if it's not connected. Then again, the principle of Sabbath rest is a very different and much deeper concept

heath

than "going to church." My point is, either way, there is no box to check off. You don't get a gold star if you make it to church enough weekends in your lifetime. If you are keeping track of your church attendance, you have a misunderstanding of God. Your church experience should be something you find helpful and encouraging.

I really believe you should be there. But if you need to pull your ox or your . . . child out of a well on a Sunday, please do so.

She Nearly Gave Up on Christianity

One of the most Jesus-like people I've ever met almost gave up on Christianity because of this problem of legalism. Mary Kamau is a woman who, alongside her husband, started a ministry to feed school-age children in the slums of Nairobi. What started as taking lunches to a few kids has since grown to serving 23,000 kids in sixteen schools around Kenya.

She told me that she first learned about Jesus in a personal way in boarding school and had committed her life to Christ. But then she got her ears pierced. *Gasp.*

> As soon as I went back to my dorm, more than ten girls, who were members of the Christian Union, came to me and questioned why I had backslidden. I was shocked and astounded at this question. They told me that piercing my ears meant I was seeking the beauty of this world. They quoted a lot of scriptures and tried to prove to me how sinful I was.
>
> I started doubting that salvation was real. It seemed like it was something many could not reach in life. I felt there

were too many dos and don'ts, which I could not cope with. At the same time, I felt like these people were selfish and had no love, because they had not taught me love. They only judged me. In fact, I had no Bible, so when they quoted those scriptures, I couldn't refer to them for myself to understand.[6]

Thankfully, Mary spent time with a cousin who really understood Jesus and could explain his hypocritical followers. I shudder to think how much good the world would have missed if Mary hadn't found a group of believers who helped her get out of the game. She didn't even understand the game, but just knew she didn't want to play.

I meet a lot of people who have never gotten over the legalists, and it breaks my heart. When people reduce Christianity to a set of rules, it makes Jesus mad.

Steve Brown wrote in *A Scandalous Freedom*:

The good news is that Christ frees us from the need to obnoxiously focus on our goodness, our commitment, and our correctness. Religion has made us obsessive almost beyond endurance. Jesus invited us to a dance . . . and we've turned it into a march of soldiers, always checking to see if we're doing it right and are in step and in line with the other soldiers. We know a dance would be more fun, but we believe we must go through hell to get to heaven, so we keep marching.[7]

Let's not lose sight of what the Bible tells us: "It is for freedom that Christ has set us free. Stand firm, then, and do not let yourselves be burdened again by a yoke of slavery" (Gal. 5:1). Remember that the famous verse you see at football games says:

For God so loved the world that he gave his one and only Son, that whoever believes in him shall not perish but have eternal life. For God did not send his Son into the world to condemn the world, but to save the world through him. (John 3:16–17)

This leaves us with only two choices. We can admit that we suck, then welcome the amazing grace of Jesus into our lives and learn to live like him because it's the best way to live. Or, we can go back to religion and the law, and continue comparing ourselves with the people around us so we can feel better about ourselves. Don't forget that the nonreligious people flocked to Jesus, and the religious people killed him.

I don't know who said it first, but:

Religion is about what God wants *from* you.
Jesus is about what God wants *for* you.

Rules don't work when you try to work them to be right with God. Homer's understanding of Christianity was that it is about well-meaning rules that don't work in real life. It can certainly seem that way in many of our churches, but it doesn't have to be. Particularly when we shift our perspectives to be in line with the Savior who played a different game.

CHAPTER 4

WHEN MORALS GET IN THE WAY

Play It Backward

"Do not judge, or you too will be judged. For in the same way you judge others, you will be judged, and with the measure you use, it will be measured to you.

"Why do you look at the speck of sawdust in your brother's eye and pay no attention to the plank in your own eye? How can you say to your brother, 'Let me take the speck out of your eye,' when all the time there is a plank in your own eye? You hypocrite, first take the plank out of your own eye, and then you will see clearly to remove the speck from your brother's eye."

(MATT. 7:1–5)

I AM A LOVER OF many kinds of music. You will rarely find me without something playing in the background. My soul operates at a different level with great music. This makes me a bit of an audiophile—I want to hear it and hear it well. That means digital, not vinyl. I can't romanticize "good ol' vinyl" and

41

tell you that I still love listening to the pops and cracks of an LP. I'm not that cool.

However, one thing you can't do as easily with digital music is play it backward. "Why would one want to do that?" you may ask. Oh, there are so many bad periods of Christian culture that many of you have missed. During the days of what we would now call "classic" rock in the late seventies and early eighties, a movement arose within Christian circles warning of the dangers of rock music. This coincided with the beginning of what we would now call contemporary Christian music.

If I can be completely honest, I don't pay a lot of attention to lyrics. I'm one of those guys driving in his car singing whatever I *think* are the lyrics, not necessarily what they really are. For the longest time, I thought the line in Zeppelin's "Stairway to Heaven" was "and there's a wino down the road." Luke Bryan also admitted on *American Idol* that he thought the Imagine Dragons song title was "Ready to Rock You," not "Radioactive." We all do it. So while I do understand that there *were* lyrics in the music I had blasting off the 8-tracks in the glove compartment of my VW Bug during high school that were not really of benefit to my spiritual life, I would argue that I wasn't paying much attention to them.

This rock music battle that took place during my youth was a big deal in Christian culture. There were people traveling the country urging us to burn our devil music (not sure why we couldn't just break them, but I guess melting vinyl is really cool to watch). The most insane part of this cultural war was that many of the so-called rock music experts were warning us of the subliminal messages embedded in these records that might make us want to worship Satan, if we played it backward.

Yes, I am serious.

Churches hosted seminars and brought in special speakers to warn the unwary public of the real agenda behind secular rock music. Evidently this phenomenon started with the Beatles' *White Album* in a song called "Revolution 9." If you played it backward, it said, "Turn me on, dead man." I'm sorry, but the song didn't make any sense playing it the regular way, so this was extra ridiculous. Nevertheless, the whole idea of subliminal messaging came to life.

To be clear, many of these musical artists were admittedly dabbling in the occult, and I would never want to make light of the effects of worshiping the Prince of Darkness. Some of the lyrics were raunchy. Many aspects of the music and, worse, the lives of many of the rock stars made it completely obvious that parents should be concerned about their children's musical tastes. I certainly would have been as a parent. But when the concern moved into the subliminal realm, which could only be heard if you could figure out how to make your turntable do something I could never figure out how to get my turntable to do, it started feeling like the modern equivalent of a witch hunt. And it promoted an even greater polarity between modern culture and the church. That's how I remember it, anyway. It was deeper than just musical taste. It felt like the church wanted me to choose between my Christian friends and my secular friends.

The Polarities of Music and Faith

On behalf of Jesus, I believe this polarity is a huge problem. I'm not down on Christian music, by the way; it helps my soul on an almost daily basis. But it's a different world today. Back then, it was very frustrating growing up inside this "culture polarity," while at the same time reading Jesus say:

> "You are the light of the world. A city that is set on a hill cannot be hidden. Nor do they light a lamp and put it under a basket, but on a lampstand, and it gives light to all who are in the house. Let your light so shine before men, that they may see your good works and glorify your Father in heaven." (Matt. 5:14–16 NKJV)

I know what you're thinking, and I agree with you that my musical choices do not necessarily affect my ability to be a light in the world. And I get that my light needs to be bright enough to see. But hide it under a bushel? No. I'm going to let it shine. My light is irrelevant if non-Christians can't see it and don't know about it. Worse yet, they won't want anything to do with it if it comes with a judgmental attitude. That's what my introduction to the culture war felt like.

In Bible college I joined a group of people and picketed a rock concert one night. I'm not proud of what I did, and actually, neither is the professor who took us. I just remember holding signs and yelling at the people in line. Some kind of judgmental stuff like, "Jesus loves you, but it's hard to hear that from my tone of voice right now, because *I'm yelling at you!*" I don't know. I just remember thinking, *This is not helping, and I'm never doing this again.*

This is the polarity of which I speak. The "run and hide" mentality that removes us from the very people we're here to engage, accompanied by the attitude of superiority and disgust.

If Christians merely have "light" parties all the time with their "light music" and their already lit friends (that probably doesn't sound like I want it to, but you know what I mean), we've failed to be disciples of Jesus, reaching out to people like he did.

> Now the tax collectors and sinners were all gathering around to hear Jesus. But the Pharisees and the teachers of the law muttered, "This man welcomes sinners and eats with them." (Luke 15:1–2)

Pay attention to the verbs. The sinners were *gathering to hear* Jesus, while the Pharisees were *muttering*. They were muttering to the crowd, not even talking directly to Jesus, referring to him as "this man."

The same thing happened when Jesus decided to hang out with a tax collector up in a tree, named Zacchaeus.

> When Jesus reached the spot, he looked up and said to him, "Zacchaeus, come down immediately. I must stay at your house today." So he came down at once and welcomed him gladly.
>
> All the people saw this and began to mutter, "He has gone to be the guest of a sinner." (Luke 19:5–7)

The word *mutter* is from the Greek *diagogguzo*, "to complain or grumble." It comes from the same root word where we get *diarrhea*, which tells you something. Basically, the muttering church leaders said to the crowd, "Mmmmuttermm, this guy, what's his name? Jesus? How can you all follow him and listen to his teaching when he welcomes sinners?" Can you picture them with picket signs? You can hear what they are saying, can't you? The very fact that the church officials put people in a category called "sinners" implies that they don't believe they themselves are sinners.

Jesus told a story that described them perfectly:

"Two men went up to the temple to pray, one a Pharisee and the other a tax collector. The Pharisee stood by himself and prayed: 'God, I thank you that I am not like other people—robbers, evildoers, adulterers—or even like this tax collector. I fast twice a week and give a tenth of all I get.'" (Luke 18:10–12)

Now we are staring into the hot magma core of the problem. Notice the list, from robbers to tax collectors. When I want to think better of myself, it helps to have a list of all the things I'm not. But let's be brutally honest, this listing exercise is a diversionary tactic. As long as we can keep the focus on them, no one is looking at us.

It's remarkable that the Pharisee actually prayed this way, let alone that he stood up to do it. What an obnoxious sense of pride and arrogance. I could picture him clearing his throat, *Ahem*, before proceeding to pray about himself. Jesus, in telling this story, is dripping with sarcasm. I'm pretty sure he imitated this guy with some kind of a snobbish British accent, saying:

Almighty God of the universe, thou who reigns on the eternal throne of the highest heaven. I have decided to grace you with my presence today. I come in gratitude today, Omnipotent One, and let me begin by thanking you that I'm awesome. I'm not sure if you had anything to do with that, O Lord, but I'll give you the benefit of the doubt. I certainly look good here next to that guy, which is why I decided to stand to greater illustrate the comparison. In case you haven't been paying attention, Mighty One, "I fast twice a week and give a tenth of all I get."

The first step in self-aggrandizement is to make a list of the people who are beneath you. The second step is to make a list of all the things you do well:

And while I'm at it, holy omniscient Benefactor, please don't forget all that I've done right: my piety, and my contributions to your account.

He sounds like someone giving money to a charity and expecting to have his name put up on a wall somewhere.

Tim Keller, founding pastor of Redeemer Presbyterian Church, says, "One of the problems with moralism—the idea that you can merit God's salvation by your good works and moral efforts—is that it is profoundly hypocritical. It cannot live up to its own standards."[1] The problem is that the Pharisee did not really go to the temple to pray; he went to inform God of his goodness. The Bible says that the intended audience of Jesus' story of the Pharisee and the tax collector was "some who trusted in themselves that they were righteous, and treated others with contempt" (Luke 18:9 ESV).

Notice the Pharisee says he fasts twice a week (Luke 18:12). The Jewish law prescribed only one fasting day per year, on the Day of Atonement. But this guy was into extra credit, so he

47

fasted twice a week. History tells us it was likely on Mondays and Thursdays, which just happened to be "market day" in Jerusalem when the town was full of people. This fasting fakery was Jesus' point in the Sermon on the Mount when he said:

> "And when you fast, do not look gloomy like the hypocrites, for they disfigure their faces that their fasting may be seen by others. Truly, I say to you, they have received their reward. But when you fast, anoint your head and wash your face, that your fasting may not be seen by others but by your Father who is in secret. And your Father who sees in secret will reward you." (Matt. 6:16–18 ESV)

Those who fasted would literally make themselves look as poor, hungry, and deprived as possible, even to the point of putting on "fasting makeup."[2] I think they probably looked like the rock group KISS (not that I ever listened to that kind of music).

What about the other guy at the temple? The tax collector with the classic rock record collection?

> "But the tax collector stood at a distance. He would not even look up to heaven, but beat his breast and said, 'God, have mercy on me, a sinner.'" (Luke 18:13)

That was probably how any tax collector would feel or *should* feel. Tax collectors were Jews who had sold out their own people, and who were setting their own prices for taxes so they could steal off the top. In their greed they were helping fund the occupying Roman forces in Palestine. There was a reason they had their own sin category in all these stories.

Notice that "the tax collector *stood at a distance*" (emphasis added). The Pharisee walked right up to the front and prayed about himself, but the tax collector stayed in the back. Why? He knew he didn't deserve to be there. Actually, as a tax collector, he was forbidden from even being in the same place as a normal Jew, so the story has to be somewhat creatively drawn. The church had already decided that if one was going to sell out his Jewish brothers and sisters, he would be treated as an outsider. As a tax collector, he was only allowed to go as far as a Gentile, back where the money changers and the animal sellers were blocking things up. This is why Jesus used a tax collector in his story, as the extreme opposite of the holy, fasting Pharisee.

Let me make up a term for the issue this Pharisee was struggling with: *gracism*. In other words, religious racism. Gracism, like racism, excludes a group of people because one group believes they are superior to another. In this case, it's not about the color of one's skin but the color of one's sin. Gracism says:

- "I only listen to Christian music."
- "I fast twice a week."
- "I think I'll stand up to pray."
- "I deserve to be with the Father, but you don't."
- "I am deserving of God's grace, but you aren't."

Again, consider the target listener of the story: "some who trusted in themselves that they were righteous, and treated others with contempt" (Luke 18:9 ESV). But please don't think this is an issue isolated to the religious elite. We all struggle here. Let's take a look at another tax collector story. What about that time Jesus invited a tax collector to become a disciple?

> As Jesus went on from there, he saw a man named Matthew
> sitting at the tax collector's booth. "Follow Me," he told him,
> and Matthew got up and followed him. (Matt. 9:9)

Imagine you are one of the guys already following Jesus, and you come upon this lousy jerk one day. This would be one of those days you want Jesus to unload on the poor soul. You want Jesus to tell him he is going to hell if he doesn't change his ways. But instead, you hear him say, "Follow me." The last two words you'd expect Jesus to say to this man. "Repent, sinner!" Yes. "You suck." Yes. "Follow me"? Never!

Historians tell us that fishermen would have been some of the hardest hit by the exploitation of the tax collectors because it was hard to hide their catch from the authorities as they pulled up to shore; their success in their business was plainly obvious, lying in the bottom of their boats. And as fishermen, Peter, Andrew, James, and John were the least likely to be fans of Jesus' inclusion of a tax collector into their band of followers. At some point, it must have dawned on them: "Wait a minute. 'Follow me' means 'Join us'! We don't want that guy with his subliminally satanic rock records hanging out with us." They may have been lowly fishermen, but on the list of "those who deserve to be with God," they were still above prostitutes and tax collectors.

Here is what gracism hierarchy would have looked like in their minds:

1. Pharisees and Sadducees
2. Teachers of the Law
3. Normal People
4. Fishermen

5. Sinners
6. Prostitutes
7. Tax Collectors
8. Cubs Fans (you can put your own spin on this one)

What I'm saying is that everyone has someone they look down on. Even fishermen. Normal people looked down on the fishermen because they smelled bad. So it must have felt good for the fishermen to have someone to dump on. I'm not sure if the prostitutes looked down on the tax collectors or vice versa, but they were both definitely lower than the regular sinners, because each was put in their own sin category every time the religious leaders made a reference.

Let's look at it this way. If Jesus added Matthew, the tax collector, to his team, it was not going to help the status of his group of disciples. I'm sure his followers were overjoyed the day he called Luke, the doctor, to join them. I'm making this up, by the way. There is no record of the disciples having these reactions. It may be that they were excited to have Matthew, because he had a fast chariot and some influential friends in the government. I'm just explaining human nature as I see it: we want to be around people who make us look better, not worse.

> Gracism says . . . "I deserve to be with the Father, but you don't."

"Maybe We'll Invite Bono"

Our church is very involved in the country of Malawi in Africa. We have witnessed a fantastic model in Rwanda, thanks to

President Kagame, who has invited the world to help fix his country, instead of just giving handouts. After reading *The Purpose Driven Life* by Rick Warren, he contacted Pastor Warren to ask if Rwanda could be the first Purpose Driven Nation. We witnessed this happening in amazing ways. So, we're partnering with Warren's Saddleback Church to take their PEACE Plan—*P*lant churches that promote reconciliation, *E*quip servant leaders, *A*ssist the poor, *C*are for the sick, *E*ducate the next generation—to the country of Malawi.

During a meeting about an all-African conference, we were trying to convene with other churches in the United States, brainstorming how to get the right people there, Rick offhandedly said, "I got a note from Bono yesterday. Maybe I'll invite him."

I said, "Um, if you can get Bono there, I think we can get any pastor to show up."

I mean, everyone wants to meet a rock star! I don't care if there are subliminal messages when you play U2 backward. Everyone wants a potential social media opportunity with Bono! It hasn't happened yet, but I'm still hopeful.

One of the greatest stories we never get to hear in the Bible is what happened after Jesus invited Matthew to join him. The Bible says, "Many tax collectors and sinners came and ate with him and his disciples" (Matt. 9:10). Jesus went to Matthew's house! Perhaps to a party at his house! But "when the Pharisees saw this, they asked the disciples, 'Why does your teacher eat with tax collectors and sinners?'" (v. 11). This is so obviously offensive and morally incorrect that the Pharisees didn't even feel the need to try to explain themselves.

"On hearing this, Jesus said, 'It is not the healthy who need a doctor, but the sick'" (Matt. 9:12). Then he said something that I take as another instance of Jesus' sarcasm: "But go and learn what this means: 'I desire mercy, not sacrifice'" (v. 13). We can't really tell if he's mad or not, but I'm guessing so. Because when he said, "go and learn what this means," to the same ones who "trusted in themselves that they were righteous, and treated others with contempt" (Luke 18:9 ESV), those religious leaders must have been offended. Even more so, since the prophecy from Hosea—"I desire mercy, not sacrifice" (Hos. 6:6)—is what they would have committed to memory since they were young. He was saying basically, "I know you *know* this scripture I'm about to remind you. Now go and figure out what it *actually means.*" A better translation of "learn what this means" could be "find out what it *is.*" They know God desired mercy. They just didn't really believe it, nor did they want to live in mercy.

In other words, Jesus was saying to them, "Up front, you need to know that the goal is not to create churches where people think of themselves as righteous and treat others with contempt. That's the exact opposite of what I want!"

Let's go back to Jesus' story about the Pharisee and the tax collector who went into church to pray. Here is the punch line: justified.

> I tell you, this man [the tax collector] went down to his house justified, rather than the other. For everyone who exalts himself will be humbled, but the one who humbles himself will be exalted. (Luke 18:14 ESV)

We may not understand all the cultural nuances of Jesus' story, but it's plain to see that Jesus couldn't have used a more drastic contrast in humanity, which makes for a better story.

Most of us don't feel like we're as conceited as this Pharisee. We don't lie awake at night and think, *Oh my, I'm such a good person.* But then again, we aren't as bad as this tax collector, either. We all probably think we fit somewhere in the middle—with perhaps a lean toward the good side.

Here is the important part, though: it doesn't matter. Being justified has absolutely nothing to do with goodness or rule-following or what music you listen to. It's the exact opposite. This is especially poignant when you consider that much of Scripture we've been reading here was penned by Matthew—the tax collector. As a matter of fact, as you watch Jesus interact with people in the Gospels, it seems like the better a person was at following the rules, the harder time they had humbling themselves before God and asking for mercy.

It would feel good for me to end this chapter right here, thinking I have it all figured out. But which category am I in? Oh yeah. The problem with pride is how easy it is to recognize it in someone else but hard to see in oneself. This is painful to think about as I ponder how the church has handled itself since Jesus went back home.

If I'm not careful at this point, as a church leader, I could easily say, "God, I thank you that I'm not like other Christians who are hypocrites and self-righteous, or even like this Pharisee. I get it. I've got it figured out. My church is *for* the sinners and tax collectors."

To which Jesus would say, "But go and figure out what this means. . . ."

Because as soon as I start putting people into categories, I start falling back into gracism. "God, have mercy on me, a sinner" (Luke 18:13).

CHAPTER 5

WHEN HYPOCRISY
GETS IN THE WAY

*Posing for Pictures That
Aren't Being Taken*

*"Woe to you, teachers of the law and Pharisees, you
hypocrites! You are like whitewashed tombs, which look
beautiful on the outside but on the inside are full of the
bones of the dead and everything unclean."*

(MATT. 23:27)

MY ALL-TIME FAVORITE JOHN MAYER song is one
of his early compositions called "Comfortable." It might be one
of my all-time favorite songs, period. It's a beautifully written
breakup song. He has a new girl, but he misses the one with
whom he felt comfortable.

According to Mayer, jumping from one relationship to
another isn't as great as it seems. There is something to be said
for the comfort of the long term. To most listeners, it's just
another sad life lesson. But the reason the song is important to
me is his description of the new girl: "She says the Bible is all
that she reads. Prefers that I not use profanity."

His friends think she's awesome because she's quite a catch. But he's not so sure. He misses the old, comfortable relationship he had with the girl in gray sweatpants, and wishes they were still together. What's worse, there is something about this new girl that bothers him more than the newness of their relationship or her literary and verbal narrow-mindedness. He sings, "She thinks I can't see the smile that she's faking. Poses for pictures that aren't being taken."

I'm on a plane listening to the song right now. I've heard it a thousand times, but my heart still breaks. It's a different kind of a breakup song to me. I feel bad for John and the former love, but I feel worse for the new girl and her entire existence. Is hypocrisy a choice? Or is it something that is thrust upon you by the expectations of other people? This relationship notwithstanding, her entire life must be uncomfortable, because she's not really living the biblical life she claims to live.

Hypocrisy is so uncomfortable.

I wish the breakup part of this song could be the breakup between this real girl and the poser she's become. Don't get me wrong. I read the Bible also, and my wife also prefers that I not use profanity. (They won't let me put smiley faces in here, so my sarcasm may be hard to read.) I just can't imagine what it's like to have to live your life as a picture-posing, smile faker—even in the presence of the man with whom you share your life.

Then again, maybe I can. This kind of hypocrisy was frustrating to Jesus for many reasons.

"Woe to you, teachers of the law and Pharisees, you hypocrites! You clean the outside of the cup and dish, but inside they are full of greed and self-indulgence. Blind Pharisee!

First clean the inside of the cup and dish, and then the outside also will be clean.

"Woe to you, teachers of the law and Pharisees, you hypocrites! You are like whitewashed tombs, which look beautiful on the outside but on the inside are full of the bones of the dead and everything unclean. In the same way, on the outside you appear to people as righteous but on the inside you are full of hypocrisy and wickedness." (Matt. 23:25–28)

Meanwhile, when a crowd of many thousands had gathered, so that they were trampling on one another, Jesus began to speak first to his disciples, saying: "Be on your guard against the yeast of the Pharisees, which is hypocrisy." (Luke 12:1)

Jesus wasn't just uncomfortable with hypocrisy. Hypocrisy made Jesus angry.

What is so difficult about this issue, and the reason I feel so sorry for John's new girlfriend, is that I'm 100 percent certain that she didn't set out to be a hypocrite. Neither did these dirty-cup, whitewashed-tomb contemporaries of Jesus. It never happens on purpose. The nature of sin in our lives always leads us to hide. When Adam and Eve first brought sin into this world, the first thing they did was hide: they "heard the sound of the LORD God as he was walking in the garden in the cool of the day, and they hid from the LORD God among the trees of the garden" (Gen. 3:8).

Hypocrisy is about hiding.

The enormous irony of the John Mayer song is that in his opening description of his new girlfriend, he says they are sleeping together. It's ironic, because if this new girl has the perspective that the Bible is good and cussing is bad, then there is no possible scenario where she should be more morally comfortable with unmarried sex than she is with someone's profane description of it.

Unless her comfort is only about what other people see. It's just a song, and it's probably not based on a real situation. But when the words are coming from a famous rock star, it gives the lyrics an interesting twist. Anyone dating a rock star knows there will be pictures, whether she's famous or not. "They" might take pictures of her not reading the Bible. "They" might actually hear her boyfriend using inappropriate language. But "they" can't really know for sure what she's doing behind closed doors. That's how hypocrisy works.

Bob Goff, author of *Everybody Always*, describes it this way:

We're told by someone what God wants us to do and not do. We're told we shouldn't drink or cuss or watch certain movies. We're told we should want to have "quiet times" in the mornings and talk to strangers about "a relationship with God." We're told we should want to go on "mission trips" and "witness" to people, and sometimes we do it even if we don't really know what the words mean—but often, just for a while. After long enough, what looks like faith isn't really faith anymore. It's just compliance. The problem with mere compliance is it turns us into actors. Rather than making decisions ourselves, we read the lines off the script someone we were told to respect handed to us, and we sacrifice our ability to decide for ourselves.[1]

So what are we called to do instead? Are we trying to match our outsides to our insides? Or vice versa?

Let's look at Jesus' instructions to us about the benefits of a clean heart:

> "Are you still so dull?" Jesus asked them. "Don't you see that whatever enters the mouth goes into the stomach and then out of the body? But the things that come out of a person's mouth come from the heart, and these defile them." (Matt. 15:16–18)

In other words, our hearts are where the real issue lies. How we appear on the outside is hugely irrelevant compared to what's inside.

Interestingly, Jesus wasn't ever angry about the defiled heart. He never yelled at the tax collectors, prostitutes, or "sinners." He did talk about sin and what a defiled heart does to a person. And he told them to "go and sin no more" (John 8:11 NKJV), but Jesus knew that we will never be well until we take off the makeup.

I do not want to be misunderstood. Trust me when I tell you that I fully understand the dangers of sin. Some well-meaning Christians may think that I'm being too light on sin as they read this book. I realize I'm walking a razor's edge between the people who want to do more to legislate morality and those who don't believe morality is even a legitimate concept. It's probably a lose-lose, but if I'm going to err, I'm with Jesus. Remember what Jesus said to the religious leaders: "It is not the healthy who need a doctor, but the sick. I have not come to call the righteous, but sinners" (Mark 2:17). Which is everyone, by the way! So let's talk about the issue of sin before we go any further.

Sin is bad. There has never been a time in my life when having a dirty cup, to use Jesus' illustration, worked well for me.

When my heart is contaminated by sin, it affects me in drastic ways. I know that if I don't wash the cup, I might get an infection or an illness. For the same reason, I try to remember to change toothbrushes after I heal from a cold or flu, so I don't run the risk of having to go through the experience all over again. Contamination on the inside is deadly, no matter what the outside looks like.

I completely agree with what the apostle Paul said about sin being slavery, prison, and death.

> But I see another law at work in me, waging war against the law of my mind and making me a prisoner of the law of sin at work within me. What a wretched man I am! Who will rescue me from this body that is subject to death? (Rom. 7:23–24)

Let me remind you that I am a pastor, which means I walk with other people through the experience of contaminated living. When I look at the collateral damage sin causes in marriages, families, and individual lives, I could never take a callous look at a life full of dead bones. I'm charged with helping people clean up the mess—and it is always a mess. There is, however, something worse than your sin: the hypocrisy about your sin.

The definition of *hypocrisy* comes from the theater. It literally means "to wear a mask." The problem with the mask of hypocrisy is that over time it becomes impossible not to believe your own pretense, your own acting. You adapt to the character in your drama. That's exactly what happened to the Pharisees. Remember our earlier verse where Jesus told the story of the standing Pharisee and the lowly tax collector? He told it to "some who trusted in themselves that they were righteous" (Luke 18:9 ESV). They sincerely believed that following the rules was enough, no matter what was going on in their hearts. Cue the theme song from the *Phantom of the Opera*.

Let me demonstrate with a funny story. A cowboy at a bar in New Mexico orders three beers and sits in the back room, drinking a sip out of each one in turn. When he finishes them, he comes back to the bar and orders three more. The bartender tells him, "You know, it starts to go flat after I draw it. It would taste better if you bought one at a time."

> There is, however, something worse than your sin: the hypocrisy about your sin.

The cowboy replies, "Well, you see, it's like this. I have two brothers. One is in Flagstaff, the other in Albuquerque. When we left home, we promised that we'd drink this way to remember the days we drank together. I drink one for each of my brothers and one for myself."

The bartender tells him that it is a nice custom.

The cowboy becomes a regular and always orders three mugs and drinks them in turn. Until one day, he comes in and orders two beers. All the regulars take notice and fall silent. When he comes back to the bar for the second round, the bartender says, "We don't want to intrude on your grief, but we wanted to offer our condolences on your loss."

The cowboy looks puzzled for a moment. Then a light dawns, and he says, laughing, "Oh no, everybody's just fine. It's just that my wife and I joined the Baptist church, and I had to quit drinking. Hasn't affected my brothers, though."

That's funny right there. I don't care what you say.

I'll talk more about beer in the next chapter, but for now let's concentrate on what made Jesus mad: hypocrisy. When people tell me the church is full of hypocrites, I have one of two responses:

1. Yep. Always has been.
2. I know you are, but what am I? (It depends on how mature I'm feeling.)

The church has always been full of hypocrites. It always will be full of hypocrites, because the church is full of people, and all people are hypocrites to some degree. Trust me, I'm a hypocrite. It's better just to admit it up front. I wear masks. Some people really believe they are honest and transparent, which, to me, just proves that they are hypocrites. It's like asking someone if they are a liar. If they say no, they just lied. They may not remember a specific lie, but they know they have lied at some point.

Do these pants make my butt look big? What did you say?

The problem with lying to myself about my own sinful, dirty cup—the problem with trusting in myself that I am righteous—is that I can't ever get better if I am not honest with myself. Alcoholics Anonymous figured this out years ago. That's why they mandate everyone to introduce themselves with their name and the qualifier, "I'm an alcoholic." They have a slogan: "You are only as sick as your secrets." That's one problem with hypocrisy.

If you are not honest with yourself, you are stuck right where you are. If you're not honest with yourself, it's a lid to your growth. When it comes to you, your Father isn't interested in your outward behavior. He wants what is best for you: "The

LORD does not look at the things people look at. People look at the outward appearance, but the LORD looks at the heart" (1 Sam. 16:7).

He already knows all the dirty and dead junk inside your heart and has zero interest in how you seem on the outside. What he desires is to make you clean, but the longer you wear the mask, the harder it is for you to see yourself clearly.

If You Can't See Yourself, You'll Never Fix Yourself

I bought a mirror one time, and it just didn't look right. My image was there, but it wasn't clear, until I happened to see a little sticker on the bottom that read, "Remove the protective plastic coating." Sometimes that film they put on new appliances and furniture is so clean and tight you don't even notice it. Sure enough, when I unpeeled the plastic, the mirror showed exactly what I looked like. Some mornings I wish I had left the plastic on, but the point is that hypocrisy is like the protective plastic coating. It protects others from seeing the real you and, unfortunately, protects you from seeing yourself. If you can't see yourself, you'll never fix yourself.

You know this to be true, because it's so much easier to identify the problems in others. We think, *Why can't they see the plastic coating?* For some of you, your family experience would be completely different if someone had the ability to tell your loved ones to face up to what *you* knew to be true. Think about how different your family would have been if your mom or dad had been honest with themselves. But they hid, then made excuses instead of taking responsibility. Or maybe you've even been a part of an intervention where a loved one couldn't deal with their own reality until they had a group of people nodding their heads in agreement at the same time. I have been in a few interventions, and I can tell you that having people you love peel off the plastic coating is not fun.

Hypocrisy leads you to continue to do the same harmful things over and over again. I love the way Portia Nelson illustrates this concept in her poem, "There's a Hole in My Sidewalk":

> **Chapter One**
> I walk down the street.
> There is a deep hole in the sidewalk.
> I fall in.
> I am lost . . . I am helpless.
> It isn't my fault . . .
> It takes forever to find a way out.
>
> **Chapter Two**
> I walk down the same street.
> There is a deep hole in the sidewalk.
> I pretend I don't see it.
> I fall in again.
> I can't believe I am in the same place.
> But it isn't my fault.
> It still takes me a long time to get out.
>
> **Chapter Three**
> I walk down the same street.
> There is a deep hole in the sidewalk.

I see it is there.

I still fall in . . . it's a habit.

My eyes are open.

I know where I am.

It is my fault.

I get out immediately.

Chapter Four

I walk down the same street.

There is a deep hole in the sidewalk.

I walk around it.

Chapter Five

I walk down another street.[2]

That can only happen if you recognize the hole. You will never stay out of the hole if you aren't honest about its existence.

Leading Others into the Pit

Speaking of holes, the worst part of hypocrisy is not the one I fall into. Matthew 15 reminds us, "If the blind lead the blind, *both* will fall into a pit" (Matt. 15:14, emphasis added).

What made Jesus mad was not what we do to ourselves in our hypocrisy, but what we do to those following us. Jesus was angry with the religious hypocrites because of what their fake show of religious piety was doing to the rest of the world: "[shutting] the door of the kingdom of heaven in people's faces" (Matt. 23:13).

It's one thing to be a hypocrite. It's another thing to be a hypocrite when you're standing on stage every week supposedly speaking for God. The problem with that hypocrisy is its distraction from who God really is and what his heart is really about. It's like a magnet that deflects the needle on the compass, causing it to point in the wrong direction. If a person can't find true north, they will be lost, "blind," as it were. People in leadership have the responsibility and the privilege to lead those who follow them toward a desired destination. When Jesus came, the followers were extremely lost, mostly because the church leaders had confused them with their hypocrisy. This made Jesus angry. We know this because of the disciples' reaction to his condemnation of the Pharisees' hypocrisy:

> Then the disciples came to him and asked, "Do you know that the Pharisees were offended when they heard this?"
>
> He replied, "Every plant that my heavenly Father has not planted will be pulled up by the roots. Leave them; they are blind guides. If the blind lead the blind, both will fall into a pit." (Matt. 15:12–14)

Boy, I hope you can see how upset Jesus was. Even the disciples saw his anger, and they were embarrassed by his strong objection to the Pharisees' hypocrisy. These disciple guys weren't exactly pillars of political correctness themselves. James and John were nicknamed the "Sons of Thunder." That doesn't sound mild-mannered, does it? So when the Sons of Thunder think you ought to lighten up, you must *really* be steaming. To Jesus, it was not a time to mince words when people were falling into pits. If the church leaders wanted to fall in, that was up to them, but people were following them!

To those of you in leadership in the church, I'm suggesting it's time for some transparency. Stop posing for pictures that aren't being taken. Lead like someone who's also fallen into the pit and knows a way to avoid it.

To those of you who have been hurt or even abused by a mask-wearing member or leader of the church, I wish it were different, and that it isn't such a common story. If that's your story, please accept my apology on behalf of the church for allowing it to happen. I don't understand why God didn't stop it from happening, but I know he didn't cause it. And we, as church leaders, should have stopped it.

To all, let's spend more time thinking about the inside, because we're only as sick as our secrets. Now, let's go back to that cowboy story and his beer-drinking dilemma.

CHAPTER 6

WHEN TRADITION GETS IN THE WAY

"A Guy Walks into a Bar . . ."

For John the Baptist came neither eating bread nor drinking wine, and you say, "He has a demon." The Son of Man came eating and drinking, and you say, "Here is a glutton and a drunkard, a friend of tax collectors and sinners." But wisdom is proved right by all her children.

(LUKE 7:33–35)

Jesus replied, "And you experts in the law, woe to you, because you load people down with burdens they can hardly carry, and you yourselves will not lift one finger to help them."

(LUKE 11:46)

Since you died with Christ to the elemental spiritual forces of this world, why, as though you still belonged to the world, do you submit to its rules: "Do not handle! Do not taste! Do not touch!"? These rules, which have to do with things that are all destined to perish with use, are

> *based on merely human commands and teachings. Such*
> *regulations indeed have an appearance of wisdom, with*
> *their self-imposed worship, their false humility and their*
> *harsh treatment of the body, but they lack any value in*
> *restraining sensual indulgence.*
>
> (COL. 2:20–23)

ONE OF MY BEST FRIENDS, Bill, grew up with a dad who was a World War II veteran and club manager of an American Legion hall. One day we were talking about Jesus and hypocrisy and legalism, and Bill told me more of his history with the church:

When I was a kid, I rode my bike all over town. Frequently, I would go down by the club and just stop in there to see what was going on, maybe bum some money, or get a coke, or whatever. I was around the club quite a bit.

Between my junior and senior year of high school, I started dating this girl, this really cute girl. I was not a Christ-follower then, but her family was. Her family was a strong example of healthy Christianity for me, which led me to Jesus, and a tough choice at the same time.

One of the big struggles I had early on was what to do with my dad and his job. I stopped going down by the club where he worked, because certain church people who were influential in my life said, "You shouldn't be there. You shouldn't be in that environment."

I wish I would have figured out that those people were just well-meaning. Although the general principle might have been true, at the same time, I missed a chance to be

Jesus to my dad. The club was the place he was most often. He didn't go to church. He wasn't going to come onto my turf as a believer. He wasn't going to show up at church one week and say, "Tell me more." That just wasn't who my dad was.

It was much later in life that I realized there was nothing "sinful" about me going down there, sitting at the bar where my dad worked, meeting his friends, seeing what he did, and just hanging out and being there.

I remember my internal what-if conversations at the time. *What if they see your car in the parking lot? What kind of witness is that going to be? What if they see you walking out of there and think you've been drinking?* It makes me sad, because . . . I would give . . . anything . . . to sit with my dad at the bar . . . one more time.

My dad came to Christ, and we were good the final years of his life. I just don't ever want people like my dad to get this sense that until they get everything lined up, Jesus has his back turned toward them. It's just the opposite. Absolutely the opposite.

What my dad needed to hear, what his friends needed to hear, was, "You know what? I know life's a mess right now. Jesus loves you. He wants a relationship with you. You can't get your life squared away on your own. It's going to be . . . three steps forward and two steps back, but we're with you in this."

"Jesus loves you" is a message that most people believe, but they think it's just because he *has* to love them, being God and all. The idea that Jesus *likes* you is different. Like he would want to hang around you, even when things are not all squared away in your life. That's honestly a more difficult message to grasp.

That Jesus would have wanted to be with me at my dad's bar. That's what the world needs to hear.[1]

I couldn't agree more, and neither could Jesus.

In My World

I hate what alcoholism does to people. I've seen alcohol mess up so many lives. I'm not sure why God made the fermentation process, or why he made plants that you can dry, smoke, and get high on. I don't know why he made mosquitoes either. But let's just, for the sake of this book, agree that he did.

Our responsibility from the beginning has been about creation management. Everyone must decide how they think God wants us to work it all out. As for me, I don't smoke pot, I kill as many mosquitoes as possible, and I occasionally drink a glass of wine. The latter is a newer part of my life. Like those in Bill's church, I grew up as a teetotaler. (Which is a word that is much more fun to say than it really should be, don't you think?)

When I was young, in my world alcohol was wrong. It was a sin. End of story. Then I moved to Chicagoland to pastor a church. Different parts of the country handle alcohol in different ways. Let's just say that Chicagoland is not known for teetotalling. I'll never forget the first time one of my church leaders offered me a beer. I was shocked. Thankfully, I didn't make a big deal out of it. I just said to myself, *Toto, we're not in Kansas anymore.*

Eventually, my wife and I came to understand the differences between the culture in which we were raised and the culture of Chicagoland. Eighty percent of the people in our area grew up in a Catholic background. They have a respect for and hunger for the Word of God, yet many of them had given up on understanding God and his love and grace.

As I adjusted to this new demographic, I softened toward Notre Dame football and got a little more used to people calling our service a mass and me "Father Tim." This change also forced me to go back and reexamine what was actually tradition versus something mandated in Scripture. And though I've found that some of what the Catholics do is not based in Scripture, some of what my conservative, evangelical theology taught me wasn't either.

This alcohol issue may seem like a waste of paper to most of you, but to Christians in many areas of the country, alcohol is taboo. Those people, like the ones in Bill's story above, taught me that alcohol was wrong. Period. I'll admit, it was always confusing to me growing up.

As previously mentioned, I was never a complacent learner, so I asked the obvious question about the wine in the Bible. What exactly was the "fruit of the vine" that Jesus passed down that long table at the Last Supper? The answer I received was that it was a watered-down wine with very low alcohol content, likely because people in those days did not have the means of water purification, so diluted wine would have been safer. The apostle Paul told his young disciple, Timothy, that he should "stop drinking only water, and use a little wine because of [his] stomach and [his] frequent illnesses" (1 Tim. 5:23).

But you can still become intoxicated on watered-down wine, right? Well, Paul's instructions were to use only a *little* wine, so there must have been a reason not to have too much. It's also the same word Paul used in Ephesians 5 when he instructed the church not to get drunk on wine, which I agree is outside the will of God for how he wants us to live. So let's go back to the watered-down argument. Normal wine is around 13–14 percent alcohol by volume, and beer normally runs 4–6 percent. Let's say the wine was watered down greatly to a mere beer level of alcohol. Can you get drunk on beer? Ever been to a major league baseball game?

Could it just have been unfermented grape juice? No. It would have been very difficult in that period in history and in that warm climate to preserve the "fruit of the vine" in such a way that it wouldn't ferment. It's not as if they had a big double-wide refrigerator like we have in the church kitchen. I happen to know from personal experience that grape juice left unrefrigerated starts to turn when you leave it out.

Then there is the issue of Jesus' very first miracle at the wedding. I have a funny picture in my files where someone switched the signs at a grocery store. They took a sign that read "Water" and moved it to the wine shelf, and the caption reads, "Jesus was here." Yes. Jesus made wine. Actually, Jesus made good wine. I mean, would Jesus make Boone's Farm or Two-Buck Chuck for his first miracle? That doesn't add up when you read that the host at the wedding said, "Wow, this is good stuff!" (John 2:9–10, paraphrased). Jesus made alcohol. Jesus drank alcohol. There, I said it.

In Luke 7:33–34, Jesus said, "For John the Baptist has come eating no bread and drinking no wine, and you say, 'He has a demon.' The Son of Man has come eating and drinking, and you say, 'Look at him! A glutton and a drunkard, a friend of tax collectors and sinners!'" (ESV). He was making a contrast between John the Baptist not drinking alcohol and his own practice, because the church leaders were accusing him of being a drunkard. Drunkenness is a sin, and Jesus never sinned, so that was a lie; nor was Jesus a glutton. But the implication is clear. Jesus made and drank wine that must have had the possibility of causing intoxication.

Listen, most Christians would agree that drunkenness is sinful, and Christ himself warns against it (Luke 12:45). There are plenty of warnings against alcohol abuse in Scripture, such as Proverbs 20:1: "Wine is a mocker and beer a brawler; whoever is led astray by them is not wise."

> Jesus made alcohol.
> Jesus drank alcohol.
> There, I said it.

There are many who would tout the health benefits of a small amount of alcohol. I've been one of them. There is evidence to that fact, but a new study published in the *Lancet* says there is no amount of alcohol that is safe for your overall health. Alcohol was linked with 2.8 million deaths in 2016.[2]

My point here is not about alcohol; it's about making up rules. It's about making it harder to connect with God. This becomes another barrier to access with the Father. That's what made Jesus mad.

The Problem Wasn't That Jesus Drank; It Was Where He Drank

Let me explain how this all fits into the theme of this book. Jesus was constantly rebuked by the church leaders of his day for being around the wrong kinds of people, and much of his angry words were directed at defending his acceptance of the wrong crowd, who had bigger problems than alcohol.

Again, as the person who helps clean up the aftereffects of alcohol abuse, I can guarantee you that the odds of having crises in your life will diminish exponentially if you leave alcohol alone. But we must decide how to weigh the potential social and health benefits of any temptation. These days those temptations may be as likely to be found at a health club or on social media as they are at a bar.

A good example is social media. It can be good, it can be bad, and it can be a temptation. We all need to decide how to manage that tension. But I don't see many church leaders railing against having an Instagram account. And yet I know what they'd say if they saw me coming out of a bar. I think Jesus would have done both—and managed them well.

Craig Groeschel is the pastor of Life.Church, the largest church in the United States. He talked about a time when he bumped into a well-known person in his area. The guy was known for making a lot of money doing very questionable things. He recognized Craig and asked if they could meet. Craig agreed, and they met at a restaurant. When he got there, the guy was at the bar drinking, and it was only lunchtime. Craig said, "As I sat down at the bar, I could feel the people all looking at me. I could feel them whispering, talking about who I was with. Wondering if that was my beer. That week, I got two phone calls to the church office, with people complaining because I was at a bar with a well-known sinner. 'Doggone it,' they'd say, 'there goes Pastor Craig acting like Jesus again.'"[3]

Jesus was a master at this. He never sinned. To our knowledge, he never even found himself in a situation where he could be accused of doing anything wrong, except for those things the Pharisees trumped up. Yet the ones who were blatantly living outside even their own knowledge of how God wanted them to live (tax collectors and prostitutes) felt accepted and loved by him. Evidently, he drank with them. Socially.

What made Jesus mad was the pharisaical attitude these church leaders had about with whom they wanted to be social. (Isn't it interesting that we now have a behavior adjective based on the name of this group of church leaders?) Jesus said basically, "I'm here to *help* people, to save people, to unburden people that you've been loading down."

"Woe to you, teachers of the law and Pharisees, you hypocrites! You shut the door of the kingdom of heaven in people's faces. You yourselves do not enter, nor will you let those enter who are trying to." (Matt. 23:13)

"And you experts in the law, woe to you, because you load people down with burdens they can hardly carry, and you yourselves will not lift one finger to help them." (Luke 11:46)

Talk about denied access. Jesus is telling these leaders that they had been literally shutting the door to the kingdom by loading people down with extra burdens, with rules like teetotalling. We've been doing the same thing, shutting the door on people who choose to drink alcohol, or break any of the other rules we've added, such as what to wear in church, which words to use, getting tattoos, and so on. They all create another barrier, another closed door to the Father.

There was a Christian phenomenon a few years ago about WWJD. People bought stickers and had bracelets and paraphernalia reminding themselves to ask, "What would Jesus do?" in whatever situation they were in. It was a great idea! I suppose a part of the point of this book is to remind us of that same thing.

After I mentioned something about WWJD in one of my sermons, Franco, one of my friends who is a biker, came up to me and told me his history with the initialism. He was not religious when WWJD started popping up all over the place. He saw a lot of guys putting the patches on their vests and thought it looked cool, so without finding out what the letters stood for, he put one on. One day he finally asked, and when he heard what it was, he said, "Oh, I always thought it was 'We Want Jack Daniels.'" I'm pretty sure nobody laughed at that more than Jesus. He would have enjoyed spending time with Franco. He does enjoy spending time with Franco.

When you watch the life of Jesus, it seems to me that he not only felt called to the sick (sinner) because he was a doctor (Luke 5:31), but he might have actually liked hanging around them more than the religious people. Would he wear a WWID (What Would I Do) bracelet?

My Own Quandary with Beer

I had a life-altering moment in a Hampton Inn in Cincinnati, Ohio, in 2007. A new friend was telling me about how his daughter and son-in-law were getting ready to start a campus ministry in Birmingham, England. From the second he started telling me about the idea, I knew it was something Jesus wanted my daughter, Rachel, to do; that is, for her to take a semester break from college and go on mission to England. I also knew that if I told Rachel about it, she was going, whether Jesus liked it or not.

My wife and I no longer associated alcohol with being sinful by this point, but obviously that did *not* include allowing our underage daughters to drink. But as we got closer to sending Rachel overseas, we were presented with a twist. The campus ministry idea was to send a good team of fully trained young adults to do logistics, find a place to live, and search for a gathering space for local students, while at the same time recruiting US college students to transfer to the local university for at least a semester. It may sound subversive, but it's difficult for us to effectively do "mission" without becoming part of the culture, like Jesus did by becoming man—the incarnation was subversive.

Even more so than in the United States, the culture of a college campus in England revolves around the pub. And the legal drinking age in Europe is much younger, maybe eleven? In any case, experience with alcohol starts much earlier in most European countries. No fake IDs needed. So the campus ministry decided, correctly, that being in pubs was the only way to make connections, and that trying to have a Coke at the pub wouldn't be enough. Not only did its members have to go to pubs, but they needed to have a drink with people—like, socially drink beer.

Rachel was only twenty. She wasn't legal to drink in the United States, but she was allowed in England. So this ministry group had to have us sign a parental authorization for her to go to pubs and drink beer. That was the strangest field-trip permission form ever! Honestly, it wasn't a hard discussion for us because of the extreme confidence we had both in this ministry and in our daughter. We weren't naive enough to think this would be her first time being around other young people with alcohol, and she was only a few months from being legal here anyway. This group had strict policies around the alcohol issue, and to my knowledge there has not been any problem with the approach.

But there has been fruit. For example, one young man, Ash, approached the group and started asking questions about faith in Jesus. For him, this little band of believers represented Jesus in a way he had never seen before. He became interested, started dialoguing with them, and eventually decided to follow Christ. I know the story well, because Rachel was a big part of that process, and because Rachel and Ash eventually started dating. He moved to Nashville, married my daughter, and is the father of two of my grandsons. I honestly don't know if it would have happened without a few pints of Guinness.

You'll have to decide for yourself how to deal with the tension of alcohol, but for me, it was worth taking the chance! Ash is now in the kingdom, and I have adorable grandchildren with really weird accents.

A Barrier Not Meant to Exist

I sometimes get the opportunity to teach young pastors, and I'll never forget the conversation I had with a young man after a session one day. He was pastoring in a small, conservative church in a small town. He told me that the demographic of his church was older, and he feared for its very existence. There were younger families in the town, many of whom were the children of the older members. But, although they were still "members" of the church, they just didn't really want to be a part of the church.

I asked him what the younger generation liked to do in their town. He said many of them were a part of the volunteer fire department, which served as both a service to the community and a pseudo-club. They liked to hang out at the firehouse and drink beer on the weekends. (Which may not instill a great deal of confidence in the fire safety of their town, but I assume they at least have a designated fireman.) So I said, "Why don't you go spend time with them at the firehouse? You don't have to drink beer with them, but you should go to them. That's what Jesus did."

I'll never forget the look on his face. I think he knew I was right, but he also knew that the leaders of his church would never stand for it. It was the same "rock and a hard place" situation that caused Jesus to end up buried in a hard place . . . with a rock in front of the tomb. There are rules and we can't break them, or we will pay.

I know a lot of believers like this. I know that, like Bill's story earlier, there are many Christians who would be uncomfortable knowing that their pastor is at a party with alcohol, even though Jesus often was. It's just impossible for me to imagine. I can't imagine one of the older members of that church knowingly allowing their children or grandchildren to miss out on a relationship with Jesus because they created a barrier to God about drinking beer, a barrier that was never supposed to exist.

I again say that what Jesus wants is for us to help connect God to his children, and what makes him mad is when we, instead of helping, end up making it harder for people to connect. I believe we tend to default here with the rules and traditions because the more rules we add, the easier it is to judge others and feel better about ourselves.

But Jesus called us to be better than this.

CHAPTER 7

WHEN JUDGMENT GETS IN THE WAY

Caught in the Act

*Jesus went to the Mount of Olives. At dawn he appeared
again in the temple courts, where all the people gathered
around him, and he sat down to teach them. The teachers
of the law and the Pharisees brought in a woman caught
in adultery. They made her stand before the group and
said to Jesus, "Teacher, this woman was caught in the
act of adultery. In the Law Moses commanded us to
stone such women. Now what do you say?" They were
using this question as a trap, in order to have a basis for
accusing him.*

(JOHN 8:1–6)

I'VE DECIDED TO GIVE NICKNAMES to my grandchildren. My oldest grandson, Charlie, is "Google Bear." He's
really smart, especially for a four-year-old, but for some reason, in ways he probably takes after his grandfather, he thinks
he knows everything. Like Google. His little brother, George

Timothy (GT), is "Mustang." Owning a Mustang GT is on my bucket list, and GT goes too fast and makes me smile. My granddaughter, Olivia, is "Princess," because, well, you'd have to meet her, and as the only girl in the bunch, she pretty much rules the kingdom. Her baby brother is Caleb. He's new, so I need to give him some time to develop before I brand him.

Nicknames can be fun, or they can be mean. How would you like this moniker, though? "The woman caught in the act of adultery." It's not a nickname, but it's the only way she is identified in the Bible. And it's been her moniker for two millennia. Actually, there are many folks in the Bible whose names we just don't know. I believe their name tags in heaven will say their names with an aka (also known as) below them.

- Fred, aka "Bethlehem innkeeper"
- Rita, aka "the woman at the well"
- Janice, aka "the woman caught in the act of adultery" (I don't know, maybe she'll just stick with "Janice" now that I think about it. She was, after all, "caught in the act of adultery.")

There is a beautiful precedent for name change in the Bible. Abram, whose name meant "exalted father," was changed to Abraham, "father of many" (Gen 17:5). The chief enemy of Christianity named Saul is someone we now refer to as the apostle Paul (Acts 13:9). And Simon was changed to Peter, which means "the rock" (John 1:42). These name changes identified a significant transformation in the person, a literal rebranding.

So let's rebrand this poor woman as Janice, and revisit her story:

Jesus went to the Mount of Olives. At dawn he appeared again in the temple courts, where all the people gathered around him, and he sat down to teach them. The teachers of the law and the Pharisees brought in a woman caught in adultery. They made her stand before the group and said to Jesus, "Teacher, this woman was caught in the act of adultery. In the Law Moses commanded us to stone such women. Now what do you say?" They were using this question as a trap, in order to have a basis for accusing him. (John 8:1–6)

This shows how much women had been degraded and demeaned by society at the time, even by the religious society. The guy is not here, although it obviously takes two people to be "caught in the act of adultery." John told us that this all happened during the Feast of Tabernacles (John 7:2), a weeklong celebration of thanksgiving for God's goodness. The people lived in tents for a week in remembrance of the way God cared for their ancestors in the desert. But only the males were actually required to participate. There is no way to know how many families came with them, but sadly there would have been potential for promiscuity, and it would have been an opportune time for prostitution.

We don't know who Janice was, but as the text tells us, the Pharisees were trying to trap Jesus into refuting the law of Moses, which required that she be stoned to death. It's possible that she was selling herself. It may even be implied that this wasn't the first time she'd been in this situation. Perhaps they just caught her, but if this was truly a trap, the only foolproof way for the plan to work would be to use a guy who was in on it. Where is the guy who volunteered as "tribute" for that job? And can we throw some rocks at him?

I feel so bad for Janice. I can't discount the "act," but she seems like a victim to me. I have a deep heart for women who have been trampled by society and have to stoop to using their bodies to survive. Maybe I'm reading way too much into this, and these church leaders just knew that someone was "carrying on" and had a secret camera. But it doesn't seem fair that there aren't *two* people standing half-naked in judgment in front of Jesus.

So, please give Janice the benefit of the doubt for a moment, and let's watch Jesus be Jesus.

Stoned

According to the Old Testament law, Janice should be stoned for the sin of adultery. Let me try to quickly answer the question some of you may be thinking at this point: *What's the deal with the Old Testament law?* Right? I mean the whole Old Testament is full of these laws, and this one seems pretty extreme, especially today.

God hasn't changed. Jesus said, "Anyone who has seen me has seen the Father" (John 14:9), and John and Paul said Jesus was God in flesh (John 1:1, 14; Col. 2:9; 1 Tim. 3:16). But sometimes the God who made up the Old Testament law doesn't sound like Jesus. I understand your concern, but I don't have the time in this book to help you figure it all out. Actually, I don't think anybody *does* have it all figured out. Nobody has God figured out. If they say they do, don't buy their book.

This is what you need to know. Jesus plainly said he came to bring a new covenant (Luke 22:20). That's the bottom line. The

God of the Old Testament may be hard to understand, so watch him work through the person of Jesus.

Janice was thrown at Jesus' feet, guilty as charged. Jesus had been teaching in the temple courts when it happened. It's so easy for me to get distracted when I'm teaching. I can't imagine trying to keep my train of thought if a hysterical, resisting, disheveled woman was dragged into the auditorium.

The Bible tells us they made her stand. (I really do not like them.) This much we know: she was in trouble, but all they cared about was using her to test Jesus. Although Jesus is not angry per se in this story, it fits into our thesis because of all the other information we have about his interaction with these hypocrites. But, hey, I'm angry for this woman, so let's do this.

This story always makes me wonder what was going through Jesus' mind. We don't have any record of it. But think about this: Jesus grew up in a town where they thought his mother had committed the same sin, because they didn't believe the miraculous virgin birth story. In at least one instance, the people accused him of being an illegitimate child (John 8:41).

When we celebrate Christmas each year, we usually take time to remember the hardships that Joseph and Mary went through as she gave birth to the Son of God, but I doubt we fully comprehend the one hardship they could *never* live down. The long trip to Bethlehem came and went, but the looks of people back home never did. Only a select few believed the incarnation story. In the eyes of everyone, Mary had broken the law: she was pregnant with Jesus out of wedlock whether with her fiancé or someone else. I believe Jesus' childhood experience gave him a unique filter as he dealt with situations like these. Prostitutes used to be referred to as "women of ill repute." Jesus' mother was a woman of "ill repute," even though she deserved the opposite reputation.

I'm honestly amazed at Jesus' composure in this situation. I don't know if you're feeling my emotion here, but if I were Jesus, I would have gone spider monkey on these guys! It's one of the reasons why I know that when Jesus *did* direct his anger, it was not an emotional reaction. He kept his emotions in check, allowing him to deal more proactively with his anger, which is something he does in every situation. Something you and I should do more often.

Adultery breaks up families, which is one of the reasons for God's harsh penalty in the first place. I know some of you would like to go spider monkey on an adulterous man or woman who broke up your own family. And I can understand that. But I still can't help but feel for Janice. She was just a pawn in a bigger chess game, a trap to capture Jesus.

What could Jesus say? If he had set her free, he'd be violating the law of Moses. If he had said to stone her, well, that's just not who Jesus was. He came to connect people to his Father; he was there to help Janice connect to her Father. The Bible says, "But Jesus bent down and started to write on the ground with his finger" (John 8:6). What did he write?

The Greek word for *write* used here is *katagrapho*, which means "making a list." With the prefix *kata*, it literally means, "to write *against*." Considering the way the men reacted, it's not likely he was writing against the woman. He was probably in some way writing against her accusers. Some have speculated that it was a list of the Ten Commandments, because in Deuteronomy 9:10, it says that when God the Father wrote the Ten Commandments, he did it with his own finger. Others have suggested that it was a list of the accusers' names. Maybe it was both; a list of their names *next* to the commandments they had broken.

Seriously, this was like challenging Santa. Jesus has the ultimate "naughty and nice" list, and he doesn't need to check it twice. "Let's see. Billy: broke commandments 2, 3, 5, 6, 7, 8. Johnny: broke commandments 4, 5, 6, 7, 8, 9, 10. . . ."

There is also another interesting speculation. Remember that these church leaders knew the Old Testament stories like the back of their hands. They didn't have Netflix back then; studying was all they ever did. So they would have known about a time in the book of Daniel when God wrote an indictment against the wicked king on the wall. Have you heard the phrase "the handwriting on the wall"? That's from when God wrote on the wall with his own hand, *Mene, Mene, Tekel, Upharsin*, part of which means "You have been weighed on the scales and found wanting" (Dan. 5:27). That could have been something Jesus scribbled in the dirt that day.

My guess is that the reason we don't know exactly what he wrote is because it doesn't matter. He may have just been doodling or starting a game of tic-tac-toe for one of the kids in the crowd. Who cares? What I want you to do is picture the situation and understand the brilliant compassion he created in this moment. Jesus was creating a diversion.

Janice was standing, after being caught in the act of adultery. Most network television programs dress women in something presentable when filming a bedroom liaison. I applaud that, but that's not usually how it works in reality. Janice likely wasn't still wearing a negligee when they busted into the room. And it's doubtful they allowed her to put on her jeans and hoodie before they dragged her out. One way or another, she was not presentable, and everyone's eyes were on her—that is, until Jesus made them look *down*.

> When they kept on questioning him, he straightened up and said to them, "Let any one of you who is without sin be the first to throw a stone at her." Again he stooped down and wrote on the ground. (John 8:7–8)

Awkward silence.

During this time of awkward quietness, conviction began to settle in their hearts: "But when they heard it, they went away one by one, beginning with the older ones, and Jesus was left alone with the woman standing before him" (John 8:9 ESV). Instead of playing their stupid game, Jesus basically said, "I think you need to check the rules and make sure you are even allowed to *play* this game. And, by the way, you're not."

A few years ago, a survey raised the question, Who deserves to go to heaven? and listed several names. A well-known former sports star who appears to have gotten away with murder took last place with only 19 percent voting to give him a shot in eternity. Mother Teresa received 79 percent. But this is what cracked me up: 87 percent of the participants believed they themselves deserved to go to heaven. We're not great at self-evaluation, are we?

In case you're wondering, the answer is, 0 percent deserve heaven, no matter how many starving kids you saved or murders you got away with: "All have sinned and fall short of the glory of God" (Rom. 3:23).

Amazingly, though, Jesus took a lose-lose proposition and turned it into a win-win. He upheld God's law, while throwing the accusation they had placed on Janice directly back on them. I'm certain the Pharisees brought this situation to Jesus knowing that he would love this woman. His greatest crime in their eyes was his love for the unworthy of society. They thought they had him in checkmate, but instead he forced them to quit the game.

Which is, by the way, what we all need to do when we start getting judgmental. We need to take our eyes off "them" and drop our rocks.

They Started for the Doors

The older ones left first. Even judgmental hypocrites can get wiser in their old age.

I love the last part of this verse: ". . . until only Jesus was left, with the woman still standing there" (John 8:9). This is exactly where I hope we all land in our spiritual journeys: alone with Jesus.

I know for some it's an incredibly difficult place to land, precisely because the church's fallback position always seems to be a place of hypocritical judgment. I hate that. And I apologize for the many, many times I've been a judgmental hypocrite. I'm sorry for all the barriers I have created between you and God. I would love for everyone to end up like Janice: no religion, no religious people, no games—just Jesus. Being alone with Jesus is a game changer. I don't care where you have been or what you've done. If you could just be alone with Jesus, it would change everything.

Once they were alone, the Bible says,

Jesus straightened up and asked her, "Woman, where are they? Has no one condemned you?" (John 8:10)

91

I love how Jesus refers to Janice. He doesn't call her a whore or a home-wrecker. What does he call her? *Woman*. Unfortunately, this translation may sound a bit derogatory to you. But that couldn't be further from the truth. The Greek word *woman* used here is better translated as "miss" or "ma'am." It's actually very respectful. And it's the same word Jesus used to refer to his own mother (John 2:4). Don't you love that? He speaks to her with dignity and respect. He speaks to her with grace and love.

> Being alone with Jesus is a game changer.

The story continues:

> "No one, sir," she said.
>
> "Then neither do I condemn you," Jesus declared. "Go now and leave your life of sin." (John 8:11)

He is saying basically, "You are a woman who is loved by both me and your Father in heaven. Leave this life and go live like *that* woman, the dignified, forgiven, new woman. Go and live that life."

I can't help but wonder how long it had been since she had a man speak to her with such love.

Everyone in the Story Is Judged

The incredibly important move Jesus made was that he did not dismiss Janice's sin. He actually addressed everyone's sin. In a way, Jesus judged everyone in the story—and then he forgave them.

I wish the hypocrites hadn't walked away, because Jesus would have forgiven them too. I know this because he did forgive them, possibly some of those exact religious leaders, after they nailed him to a cross. As he said on the cross: "Father, forgive them, for they do not know what they are doing" (Luke 23:34).

But Janice's accusers didn't want Jesus' forgiveness. And Janice never actually asked for forgiveness either. So imagine what he wants to do for you. Romans 8:1 tells us, "Therefore, there is now no condemnation for those who are in Christ Jesus." This is a precarious concept. Forget about the believability of this kind of forgiveness; that's another issue in and of itself. There's something deep down inside all of us that wants to deserve to "go to heaven," regardless of what that might mean to us, or what that might *actually* mean, period. Deep down in our souls, the idea of free grace is not just hard to believe, but we believe it to be unfair. How could there be justice when a criminal on a cross, being executed for his crimes, turns to Jesus and asks to be "taken into the kingdom" and is granted that kingdom without question?

Say what you will, but this is the conundrum of grace: I shouldn't have to be perfect to be rewarded with a wonderful, eternal future. But, at the same time, *bad* people shouldn't be rewarded at all. People will always want to feel like they had some part in their salvation. This issue was part of the Catholic Church's basis for a *mortal sin*, a willful violation of God's law leading to the spiritual death of the soul, versus a *venial sin*, or a slight sin.

It's hard for us to put a liar in the same category as an adulterer. It just doesn't make sense to us. But grace doesn't make sense, which is what makes this story so significant.

CHAPTER 8

WHEN GRACELESS RELIGION GETS IN THE WAY

Caught in the Act Redux

IF YOU HAPPEN TO BE reading the passage about the woman caught in the act of adultery (whom I've named Janice) in a Bible or an app that has footnotes, you may have seen this statement: "The earliest and most reliable manuscripts do not have John 7:53–8:11." And some of you may have heard the popular statement about the Bible, "There are so many versions and discrepancies."

Yes, there are versions, or more accurately, translations of the Bible. It was written a long time ago in several languages that the average modern person can't understand. So, we need these translations. If you understand that up front, it shouldn't be a problem. And yes, there *are* some discrepancies. These documents were hand copied, and we don't have the original texts with perfect copies.

There is a story told of a new young monk who arrives at the monastery and, as with all new monks, is assigned to help copy the old texts of the church by hand. He notices, however, that all the monks are copying from copies, not from the original manuscript. So he goes to the old abbot and points out that if someone made even a small error in the first copy, it would never get corrected. In fact, that error would be transferred onto all the subsequent copies.

To this the abbot says, "We have been copying from the copies for centuries, but you make a good point, my son."

So the abbot goes down into the dark caves underneath the monastery where the original manuscripts are archived in a locked vault that hasn't been opened for hundreds of years. Hours go by and nobody sees the abbot. So the young monk gets worried and goes downstairs to look for him. He sees the abbot banging his head against the wall and wailing, "We missed the *r*, we missed the *r*." His forehead is all bloody and bruised, and he is crying uncontrollably.

The young monk asks the abbot, "What's wrong, Father?"

With a choking voice, the abbot replies, "The word is *celebrate*. Not *celibate*!"

I can assure you that none of the minor variations in the Scripture makes any theological difference. It's not like one copy says, "Jesus died on a cross," and another says, "Jesus went surfing." But what about Janice's story? Was it made up later by a bunch of adulterers? Or is this footnote a testament to the improbability of grace?

According to William Barclay, Scottish author and minister, only one early manuscript records this encounter. Six of the earliest manuscripts of John's gospel do not include this story; two of them actually have a blank space where it should have been. In biblical interpretation, the next step would be to look at historical evidence about the text. There is an account from an early church historian who lived just after John's time, where he mentions this story very early in church history.

The really fascinating piece of this puzzle comes from the words of one of the most respected early church fathers, Augustine. He says this story was removed from the text to "avoid scandal."[1] Which would explain the blank space, wouldn't it?

According to Augustine, and a whole lot of Christ-followers over the years, this story made Jesus look too complacent about sin, especially a *mortal* sin like adultery.

Could Grace Be As Simple As That?

The blank space dispute may be telling us something very important about religion and humanity. Perhaps Jesus' disdain for judgmentalism wasn't limited to the Jewish church of his generation. Janice's story is completely congruent with other instances of Jesus and his grace, not to mention the other parables we know Jesus did tell. It reverberates, as with all his teaching, against the anger Jesus showed to the church leaders for thinking they were better than everyone else. Maybe we've not learned enough from the angry red letters in our Bible.

Now back to our story. After everyone had left, Jesus stands up and asks Janice,

> "Woman, where are they? Has no one condemned you?"
>
> "No one, sir," she said.
>
> "Then neither do I condemn you," Jesus declared. "Go now and leave your life of sin." (John 8:10–11)

Neither do I condemn you. That's the scandal. It can't be that easy! He then said, "Go now and leave your life of sin." But he should have said this *first*, and then, when he was positive she understood the thing she had done wrong, pat her on the back and say, "Now, it's okay. I still love you." Obviously, any good parent would add, "Just don't do it again, or you know what will happen."

Could she ever really go and leave her life of sin? There is no way this woman was not going to sin for the rest of her life. Arguably, even the most spiritual man in the post-Jesus first century, the apostle Paul, said he *was*—like *currently*, as he was writing his epistles—the chief of sinners (1 Tim. 1:15). The apostle John also said, "If we claim to be without sin, we deceive ourselves and the truth is not in us" (1 John 1:8).

It is the "life of" sin Jesus was calling Janice out of. What Jesus was saying is that as a forgiven person she should make some changes in her life, leaving her old life behind. He was saying basically, "Your old life keeps you from being who God meant you to be. It hurts other people. So go now and start over." Janice could not have done that without forgiveness.

Bob George, author of *Classic Christianity*, writes,

Imagine that you own a fine cafeteria. One day, you hear this tremendous commotion out in the alley where the garbage dumpsters are. You open the back door to see what's going on, and you see the most pitiful-looking human being you have ever seen in your life—me—fighting with several stray cats over the food scraps in the dumpster. I am a virtual living skeleton. It's obvious that I am living on the edge of starvation, and probably have been for a long time. There is nothing about me to provoke liking or affection in you, but you are moved to pity. "Hey, hey!" you yell. "Get out of the garbage. Don't eat that stuff! Come over here." I trudge over to you, half-seeing you through hopeless eyes. "Listen," you say. "I can't stand to see you eating garbage like that. Come into my cafeteria and eat."

"But I don't have any money," I reply.

"It doesn't matter," you say. "My chain of restaurants has done very well, and I can afford it. I want you to eat here every day from now on, absolutely free of charge!"

You take my arm and lead me inside the restaurant. I cannot believe my eyes. I have never seen a cafeteria line before. With huge, unbelieving eyes I stare at the spread: vegetables . . . salads . . . fruits . . . beef . . . fish . . . cakes . . . pies . . . In my wildest dreams, I have never even imagined that such things could be. I look at you intently.

"Are you saying I can eat anything I want?"

"Yes, anything."

"Really, anything I want?" I ask again.

"Yes, I said anything you want," you answer.

Then slowly, with a gleam in my eye, I ask, "Can I eat some garbage?"[2]

Who would do that?

Jesus was telling Janice, "Either way you are free. You can go and start over. Those guys can't condemn you. They are sinners. They were deceiving themselves until I called them out just now. I'm the only one who can condemn you, *and I refuse to condemn you*. Go now. . . ." Jesus was trying to help her look forward, which she could only do with a clean start.

It's the same with us. Jesus is not worried about what we've done; he's forward-thinking. He loves us too much to let us keep living the way we have been, but he knows that we can't "get better." We can only "start over."

Let's go back to Janice's story and the penalty for sin. The early church appears to have deleted her story, and it's getting confusing. The question on the table is, Why could Jesus forgive her of her sin and let her go on her way without invoking the Old Testament penalty of death?

> He loves us too much to let us keep living the way we have been, but he knows that we can't "get better." We can only "start over."

Answer: he didn't. He paid for it. "God made him [Jesus] who had no sin to be sin for us, so that in him we might become the righteousness of God" (2 Cor. 5:21).

What this means is, because that woman committed adultery with that man, Christ hung on the cross, bleeding, broken, and dying. That's why he was there. She put him there. So did I. So did you.

The Gospel Says You Can't Be Good Enough *and* You Can't Be Bad Enough

You can't be good enough to win God's favor, and you can never be bad enough to miss it. The pressure is off. The Old Testament law will be upheld, and justice will be served. Jesus can love Janice. He can give her the opportunity to leave her life of sin and go live a new eternal life because he paid for it.

At this point in writing, I was talking with my daughter Lauren about the difficulties of explaining the holidays to Olivia, her three-year-old daughter. She said, "You know, explaining Christmas to a three-year-old is not that hard. Easter is a different story." She meant that explaining how Jesus died and rose again is PG-rated, and Olivia needs to know that there is life beyond this body because stuff happens and bodies wear out. But explaining why Jesus *had to* die and who put him there is a little too adult to explain. It's at least PG-13.

Jesus traded places with us. As it says in Scripture, "The wages of sin is death" (Rom. 6:23). This means any sin, even the little *venial* ones that make us believe we're better than someone who's committed the *mortal* ones.

Hey, maybe you, my dear reader, didn't get paraded into church by a mob, but you're still busted. We all are. God knows what's on the inside, and I'm pretty sure we're all adulterers, because according to Jesus, "anyone who looks at a woman lustfully has already committed adultery with her in his heart" (Matt. 5:28). He said it doesn't matter if you've actually committed the act. If you've done it in your heart, it's the same thing.

As mad as I am at these church leaders and what they did to Janice, truth be told, these horrible people who trapped and exposed her did her a great favor. They obviously didn't intend it that way; they didn't care about her at all. But they ended up leading her to a place of grace.

My friend Mark Jones brought up a great question. How did it ultimately turn out for Janice? There is so much we don't know. If she had made a habit of adultery, was already a "woman of ill repute" as it were, this encounter with Jesus had to have been a remarkable moment of acceptance in her life. However,

I'm sure the ill repute didn't go away. She probably still had to live in Jerusalem with her scarlet letter. Jesus' acceptance and forgiveness were part of the equation, but what did the church do with Janice? Or better yet, what *does* the church do with the Janices of the world?

It is important to note that at the end of the story, Jesus is down in the dirt with Janice. He is not standing up with rocks in his hands like the religious leaders. He is down at her level. What about us?

I can't explain it, but it seems as though gravity works differently for Christians than it did for our Leader. Usually the longer we follow Jesus, the more likely we are to stand, instead of getting down in the dirt—even though we know the gravitational force for Jesus always pulled him down to the lowest possible place.

> Have this mind among yourselves, which is yours in Christ Jesus, who, though he was in the form of God, did not count equality with God a thing to be grasped, but emptied himself, by taking the form of a servant, being born in the likeness of men. And being found in human form, he humbled himself by becoming obedient to the point of death, even death on a cross. Therefore God has highly exalted him and bestowed on him the name that is above every name, so that at the name of Jesus every knee should bow, in heaven and on earth and under the earth, and every tongue confess that Jesus Christ is Lord, to the glory of God the Father. (Phil. 2:5–11 ESV)

Every knee should bow. We should all bow. And only then, maybe, could we look around and see who else is down here.

CHAPTER 9

WHEN PREJUDICE GETS IN THE WAY

Woman at the Well,
Wrong Side of the Tracks

As the time approached for him to be taken up to heaven,
Jesus resolutely set out for Jerusalem. And he sent
messengers on ahead, who went into a Samaritan village
to get things ready for him; but the people there did not
welcome him, because he was heading for Jerusalem.
When the disciples James and John saw this, they asked,
"Lord, do you want us to call fire down from heaven to
destroy them?" But Jesus turned and rebuked them. Then
he and his disciples went to another village.

(LUKE 9:51–56)

IN LUKE 9, JESUS REBUKED the disciples when they
wanted to call fire down on people who did not welcome them.
Was he mad at his followers? I can't tell you for sure either way.
He might have gently said, "Um, no, kids, let's not blow them
up." I don't know. But this incident seems like it fits into our
fuller discussion.

The whole scene cracks me up. Where were James and John going to get this "fire from heaven"? I mean, they did get to heal people and cast out demons, but their superpowers were always limited to helping people, right? It wasn't like they were X-Men all of a sudden.

We don't know what Jesus said, or how mad he was. But we do know the problem. It was way too easy for the disciples to jump straight from "Let's have a Jesus party in this town" to "Let's obliterate them." Why? There was always an issue when it came to "the Samaritans." Samaria was a region most Jews avoided. For the disciples and most of Jesus' audience, Samaritans were the people on the "other side of the tracks." They had a religious system that was a form of Judaism, but they had pulled away and had come up with some of their own rules, like towns with a First Baptist and a Second Baptist. Just kidding. It was much deeper than that. Truth is, the disciples didn't want to be in Samaria, even with Jesus. They were prejudiced.

I spent my adolescent years in Enid, Oklahoma. Legend has it that before it was named, the area was just a stop on the highway. There was nothing but a restaurant by the side of the road for truck drivers. One truck driver saw the word *enid* in his rearview mirror as he drove away (*dine* in reverse), and so he named the town accordingly.

I lived on the east side of Enid and attended Longfellow Junior High, one of three junior high schools that all fed into one large high school. In terms of a small-town class system, Longfellow was usually in the middle when it came to socioeconomics, sports, and competition in whatever arena. The newer and nicer area of town was the west side. Those kids went to Waller Junior High. It felt like the Waller kids were a little uppity toward the rest of us when the school system brought us all together at Enid High School. But the great thing about being in the middle is that if we felt belittled by them, we could always look down our noses at the kids from Emerson, on the north side.

I love small towns. I loved where I lived. But can I point out the literal *small*-mindedness in this equation? I mean, we all love to compare and make ourselves feel better, but whether we lived on the east side or the west side, we all still lived in Enid! The people in Oklahoma City looked down on us, the people in St. Louis looked down on the Okies from Oklahoma City, the Chicagoans looked down on the St. Louisans, and the New Yorkers looked down on . . . well, everyone. Let's just be honest.

What I'm saying is that the world is dumb. Looking back on freshman year at Enid High School, it seems silly to me to even think about the comparisons and prejudices I engaged in and encountered. Just as it must have seemed to Jesus when the disciples revealed their own.

Jesus and Perspective

I may not actually ask God to send fire down from heaven on a group of people, but the older I get, the more I realize I wrestle with this issue of prejudice. I have much to learn, and much to teach my church, about how we interact with people who aren't like us. Let's take a look at another Samaritan story for hints as to why Jesus needed to rebuke his disciples' attitudes, and how we can keep from making the same mistake.

He had to go through Samaria on the way. Eventually he came to the Samaritan village of Sychar, near the field that

Jacob gave to his son Joseph. Jacob's well was there; and Jesus, tired from the long walk, sat wearily beside the well about noontime. Soon a Samaritan woman came to draw water, and Jesus said to her, "Please give me a drink." (John 4:4–7 NLT)

Honestly, this Jesus encounter would have been more difficult for the church leaders to wrap their heads around than the ones involving tax collectors and prostitutes. But the leaders never found out, because they wouldn't be caught dead in Samaria.

This "other side of the tracks" wasn't really a socioeconomic barrier. Everyone was poor in those days, unless they worked for the Romans in some way. It was a socio-*religious* barrier. This separation was much deeper than thinking your school is better than another. Like I said, both Jews and Samaritans claimed to be descendants of Abraham, but they didn't follow the same laws and customs.

To say that Jesus "*had to* go through Samaria" is an enormous statement of irony. Going through Samaria was certainly the shortest route from Judea up to Galilee, but most Jewish people didn't do that. They usually went out of their way to avoid passing through that region. This is more than me avoiding Wrigleyville because I'm not a Cubs fan. It's probably deeper than even a racial or socioeconomic barrier. Samaritans practiced a twisted form of Judaism. There is always a deeper level of contempt for someone who contaminates something you hold dear. Picture Britney Spears's version of "I Love Rock and Roll." Yes?

If Jesus *had to* go through Samaria, it was not for earthly reasons. It was a mission of reconciliation. Just to make sure I'm clear here, Jesus came to provide salvation for Samaritans, not annihilate them. Interestingly, this conversation is one of the longest dialogues Jesus had recorded in the Gospels, and it is with a *Samaritan woman.*

Let's look at the Scripture again: "Soon a Samaritan woman came to draw water, and Jesus said to her, 'Please give me a drink'" (John 4:7 NLT). Jesus would not have had a way to draw his own water, so his request should not have been interpreted as rude. This was like Jesus sitting down at the table in the break room and asking, "Could you pass me the salt?" The point is that he sat down at the table with *her* in the first place. It was unheard of in his day.

From her reaction, we see that this was way beyond the norm: "She said to Jesus, 'You are a Jew, and I am a Samaritan woman. Why are you asking me for a drink?'" (John 4:9 NLT), which was basically, "I can't believe you would sit here with me." Did you catch that? She was shocked to realize that someone who claimed to follow a different interpretation of God would put aside his prejudices and have a conversation with her. She must have felt a little uncomfortable. At the same time, it seems to me that she was like someone you meet from time to time, who you didn't know was lonely until you made a simple gesture of kindness. You open the door for them or just say hello, and all of a sudden you see that they needed a friend.

Note the drastic contrast in this situation. Normally a Jew would not talk to a Samaritan. Period. Add to that the fact that a rabbi would *never* talk to a woman in public; doing so was gossip worthy. And she was not just a woman, but a woman no one wanted around. How do we know? The only rational reason she would have been at the well in the middle of the day when it was hottest was because she didn't want to deal with the judgment of other people. This is like someone going to the grocery store in the middle of the night to avoid people.

It was the custom of the day that the women of a town would go to the local well at sundown when it was cooler. Perhaps this was the beginning of the tradition of "happy hour." They had to draw water anyway, so why not do it with everyone else and have some fun? They could help each other and catch up on current events. But this woman was alone in midday. Was she not welcome at happy hour?

Maybe she had other reasons for being alone. Maybe she couldn't come in the evening because she had other things to do. Maybe she just really needed water and couldn't wait until evening. But as you read on, I think you will see more of why my "not welcome" theory is correct.

What Jesus did next needs to be set up. If you read this wrong, you will think Jesus is calling her out:

"Go and get your husband," Jesus told her.

"I don't have a husband," the woman replied.

Jesus said, "You're right! You don't have a husband—for you have had five husbands, and you aren't even married to the man you're living with now. You certainly spoke the truth!"

"Sir," the woman said, "you must be a prophet." (John 4:16–19 NLT)

Let's talk more about perspective. Perspective was my problem in Enid, Oklahoma; it was the disciples' problem with the potential bombing earlier in this chapter; and it's most people's problem with this story in John 4. I have taught and preached this verse with the same preconceived judgment with which you are probably interpreting it right now. We all have our own prejudices. As Steven Sample, the author of *The Contrarian's Guide to Leadership*, pointed out, "No matter how hard he tries, a single human being can never give you a completely unbiased report on any event or issue; he will always give you a view that is filtered to some extent through his own prejudices."[1]

The revelation of the Samaritan woman having been divorced five times and currently living with a guy who is not her husband makes it sound like Jesus is calling out her lifestyle situation. At first blush it seems like an old-school hellfire preaching approach to sharing the good news. I've often heard the expression, "They can't know about the good news unless they hear about the bad news." That would be the approach of the street-corner preacher with a sandwich board and a megaphone, yelling at people for all the things they've done wrong, and telling them they are going to hell. Is that what Jesus was doing? Well, she didn't give the kind of response you would expect if she'd heard it that way. She said, "You must be a prophet," not "What business is it of yours?"

My daughter Lauren had a professor in college who grew up in the developing world. As he taught from this passage, he asked, "Why do American pastors always assume this woman was immoral? She was a woman who lived in a culture where she couldn't take care of herself. She had to live with a man in some way. Having five husbands and living with a guy does not mean she was immoral."

We desperately need recognition of the lens we look through, which may not take into account other people's realities. This is so important for followers of Jesus as we interact with people, especially with those from Samaria or whatever you want to call the other side of your tracks, or those from backgrounds and cultures we don't fully understand. For Jesus, they were people like this Samaritan woman; for me, they would be anyone other than a white male who grew up in Oklahoma forty years ago. We will never break down the barriers that exist between the Father and his children until we get past our own perspectives.

In case you haven't looked at the picture on the back of this book, I'm white. I have a white perspective. I don't remember feeling like we had a big problem with racial inequality in Enid, Oklahoma. My problems were all about which junior high school someone attended. As I think back though, I realize that, in my mind, we were over the racial thing by the late seventies. But the problem with that perception was that I am white, and so I didn't have the experiences my nonwhite friends had. I have not had many experiences where I walked into a room as the only white person; it's just not the same if you're in the majority. I'm sure the kids from Waller Junior High didn't think there was a problem in Enid either. It's different when you live at the top of the food chain.

> We will never break down the barriers that exist between the Father and his children until we get past our own perspectives.

The more life I live, the more I realize I hardly have any idea what it's like to be really oppressed. Don't get me wrong, I haven't lived a life of charm; I've got my own stories. It's just that I always had opportunity. I think it's important to admit that fact if I'm ever going to be Jesus to the world around me, and don't want to be rebuked by him.

Recently, after yet another bout of racial tension in our

country, I began teaching my congregation what I thought was a thorough Christian defense of racial equality, despite what had been presented before by prominent people who called themselves Christians. I felt deeply about the issue and thought I addressed it convincingly. So did my other middle-aged Caucasian friends when I asked about it. But then I talked to an African American friend, and he said, "I don't think you went far enough." So I gave it another shot the next week.

The problem was my lens and how I read this passage of Scripture through it. I'm guessing it's the same for you as well. As I've read about this woman at the well, I've always just assumed this woman was some Hollywood personality who couldn't stay married to one guy. So when Jesus mentioned the five-husband deal, I've always assumed he was just "setting the record straight" with someone who needed a better handle on commitment. The problem was, my assumption would only be likely in the twenty-first-century United States, where she definitely did *not* live.

If she had been divorced five times, it is most likely that she had been dumped by a husband five times, because in her time and place, she didn't have the right to divorce a husband. Unfortunately, there are still places today where women are not valued and have no rights, which is why my daughter's professor had a different perspective. In Jesus' time, it didn't matter where a woman lived; she had zero rights. She couldn't divorce a man or get a job. And there was no welfare system, so she literally had to have an "arrangement" with a man to survive. This is exactly why the early church was instructed to care for widows and orphans.

I believe this Samaritan woman's reaction to what Jesus said shows that she wasn't feeling judged at all, but rather she was feeling *known*. She didn't say anything in response except, "You must be a prophet," and then proceeded to ask him a follow-up question that showed her interest in this man who seemed to have an inside track on God, being that he knew so much about her.

If I process this scene in light of Jesus' normal *modus operandi*—like his "neither do I condemn you" reaction to Janice—the rest of the story makes a lot more sense. In my mind I've always seen Jesus with a stern look on his face, scraping one finger over the other at her while shaming her with the fact that he knows she's "been around." But now I try to picture Jesus in a compassionate Savior mode, saying, "You've had five husbands dump you, and your life is hard."

Scholars say the most likely reason this woman was passed from one guy to another in her day would have been because of her inability to have children. A woman's highest value in the first century was childbearing. Again, I'm reading more into this than is given in Scripture, and these assumptions are not really important to the point of the story, but what if? Wouldn't that change your perspective even more? All of a sudden, this woman transforms from an immoral and undeserving person to someone we'd all agree deserves the love of Jesus in every way possible. It's all about perspective.

I've had many conversations with close friends who were unable to conceive, and I realize the pain is very deep no matter what century we live in. Then again, it's head knowledge for me, because my wife and I did not have this problem. So you can add that to my list. I'm a white male from Oklahoma who did not suffer from infertility.

The reality, either way, is that this is likely a woman who

had suffered deep pain, no matter the reason she had been married and divorced five times. Doesn't that change this whole scene for you? Sure, maybe she was seriously unfaithful. Maybe she was a bad man-picker; it's not hard to imagine that a woman could do that five times. But that would still be painful. I just want us to be open to the fact that you and I don't live where she lived. An admitted lack of understanding ought to be the basis of all our interactions.

Jesus was able to start the conversation with understanding, while still addressing the elephant in the room. He started where she was by saying, "Look, I get where you are, and it doesn't matter. I want to offer you my friendship. I want to offer you living water. I know you are a woman, and a Samaritan, and I know that your past and current living arrangements may make you want to avoid people in general—but I'm not like that. God is not like that." He didn't preach at her; he acknowledged her situation.

He didn't have to affirm or deny her situation, because it was irrelevant. Jesus led with love, and he really did know her backstory. We don't. It's the perfect illustration of Romans 5:6: "When we were utterly helpless, Christ came at just the right time and died for us sinners" (NLT).

Let's return to the story. After Jesus told her about her five husbands, the Samaritan woman's natural reaction was to test Jesus' sincerity. "'Sir,' the woman said, 'I can see that you are a prophet. Our ancestors worshiped on this mountain, but you Jews claim that the place where we must worship is in Jerusalem'" (John 4:19–20). She brought up their religious differences. There is almost always a wall to break through when it comes to Jesus. I can't tell you how many times I've messed this up.

Watch Jesus minimize the differences and help her see hope instead of division:

> "But the time is coming—indeed it's here now—when true worshipers will worship the Father in spirit and in truth. The Father is looking for those who will worship him that way. For God is Spirit, so those who worship him must worship in spirit and in truth."
>
> The woman said, "I know the Messiah is coming—the one who is called Christ. When he comes, he will explain everything to us."
>
> Then Jesus told her, "I AM the Messiah!" (John 4:23–26 NLT)

This is a beautiful response! Jesus could have jumped on the argument and told her that he *did* believe Jerusalem was the correct place for the temple and her ancestors were living in error, since from Jesus' Jewish perspective that was the case. The Samaritans were not following the law correctly.[2] But Jesus decided to focus on the future, rather than debate differences.

If you think I'm taking an overly lenient approach to this conversation, let me assure you that the proof of my interpretation is in John 4:26, when Jesus tells her, "I AM the Messiah." Up to this point, other than to his closest followers, Jesus had not revealed the full extent of his identity. To the world, he was a great teacher. He wanted to have plenty of time to help his followers learn and grow, and he wasn't ready for the rebellion and revolution that claiming to be the Messiah would create. He *never* threw around the *M* word. But he told his secret to a Samaritan, to a woman who had five ex-husbands, and he welcomed her into a relationship with himself and the Father. *Bam!*

Then the disciples, who had gone to the village to buy food, returned:

> Just then his disciples came back. They were shocked to find him talking to a woman, but none of them had the nerve to ask, "What do you want with her?" or "Why are you talking to her?" (John 4:27 NLT)

Do you see it now? The prejudice? They wanted to ask him,

- "What in the heck are you doing, Jesus?"
- "Should we call down fire from heaven?"
- "Don't you realize this is a woman, a *Samaritan* woman?"
- "Don't you realize that she is here in the middle of the day, probably for a reason?"
- "Are we not uncomfortable enough being here in Samaria in the first place that you have to be here with *her*?"

I've always wondered why all of Jesus' disciples had to go into town to buy food. It sounds like the beginning of a bad joke: "How many disciples does it take to carry lunch?" I think maybe Jesus sent them away. He knew he was going to meet this woman, and he knew having his disciples around was going to make it hard for her to talk with him. From their shock, it's obvious that they would have been uncomfortable being around her, let alone speaking to her, which would have created a barrier.

My theory is backed up by the fact that as soon as the disciples showed up, she left, as if she could read their reaction.

I don't want to overstate this, but the disciples would have been in the way. Jesus' disciples often get in the way. That's the point of this book.

But when people really meet Jesus—and his followers quit getting in the way—outsiders will come streaming to him.

> The woman left her water jar beside the well and ran back to the village, telling everyone, "Come and see a man who told me everything I ever did! Could he possibly be the Messiah?" So the people came streaming from the village to see him. . . .
>
> Many Samaritans from the village believed in Jesus because the woman had said, "He told me everything I ever did!" When they came out to see him, they begged him to stay in their village. (John 4:28–30, 39–40 NLT)

This was a woman who chose to go to the well at a time when no one else went to the well, seemingly to avoid people. She was either bad at relationships or had been kicked to the curb multiple times. She was living with a man with whom she was not married. She didn't understand the correct way to worship God. And she was the first missionary to the people of Samaria.

How many mission boards would approve that? Well, in her defense, she was tight with Jesus. It was maybe just for an hour, but in that short amount of time he had revealed his true nature to her. Could it be that simple? If Jesus could look past the big issues of religious error and an unfortunate living arrangement, why can't we?

It's usually not even the big things that cause many of Jesus' followers to create barriers. It's the small stuff.

116

CHAPTER 10

WHEN NEIGHBORS AND GNATS GET IN THE WAY

Neighbors and Gnat Strainers

"Woe to you, teachers of the law and Pharisees, you hypocrites! You give a tenth of your spices—mint, dill and cumin. But you have neglected the more important matters of the law—justice, mercy and faithfulness. You should have practiced the latter, without neglecting the former. You blind guides! You strain out a gnat but swallow a camel."

(MATT. 23:23–24)

PLEASE TELL ME THERE ARE some Monty Python fans among my readership. Can't you see Jesus up on the castle wall, with a French accent, taunting King Arthur with this scripture from Matthew 23?

Imagine Jesus saying, "Woe to you—you—you dill tithers. (You must use a bad French accent to mimic the French guard's voice.) Your mother was a hamster, and your father smelt of elderberries. You hypocrites! You blind guides! You strain out a gnat but swallow a camel."

"Is there someone else we can talk to?" the Pharisees ask.

"No. Now go away, or I will taunt you a second time," replies Jesus.

This doesn't sound like happy Jesus, does it? Why? Because the Pharisees are hypocrites, blind guides. They follow all the little laws but miss the big point, neglecting justice, mercy, and faithfulness.

Gnats and Camels

The gnat was the smallest of unclean beings and was forbidden to be eaten by law. I have no idea why they would be listed. Were gnats ever a delicacy? How many gnats does it take to acquire a true flavor? I hear they have an earthy bouquet, with a leathery finish, but I'm no sommelier.

May I help you process the sarcasm and frustration of Jesus in this passage? These church leaders were legalistically obedient to the extent of literally straining their wine or water through a cloth to avoid the possibility of accidentally breaking the gnat law. Not that avoiding insects is a bad thing. It was their motive that stunk, or actually, it was the actions that accompanied the motive. They were straining gnats while engaging in religious activity that was grossly unjust and ungodly, aka swallowing the camel. Jesus couldn't have made a larger contrast in missing the point.

Straining a tiny gnat meant tithing mint, dill, or cumin. The tithe was one-tenth of the harvest, which was to be given to God; that is to the priests and Levites (Num. 18:20–24; Deut. 14:24–29). The Pharisees would go so far as to pay tithes on the tiny garden herbs used for flavoring food, some of which were about the same size as a gnat. This painstaking process should demonstrate the problem. It causes me to wonder if the idea of following the law so microscopically was about an attempt to follow the law accurately, or an attempt *not* to give God any more than was required.

Since this is a challenge from Jesus about missing the point, I want to give the Pharisees a break, because in their way they were trying to follow the law and help other people do the right thing. But Jesus was angry with their legalism, because the time and effort wasted straining and counting seeds could have been used to do something positive toward their fellow man.

Elias Chacour, the author of *Blood Brothers*, writes about growing up in a Christian boarding school in the Middle East. He went to the chapel to pray one night and fell asleep, and he was punished for breaking curfew rules even though he was in the chapel to pray.

> For the first time, I stood face-to-face with the unbending rules of the church as an institution. I could not understand why strict obedience to a rule was more important than a heart seeking God. Unhappy though I was, I could not fault the principal. He was just a man carrying out his job to the best of his ability. In the end I submitted, more or less quietly, to my punishment: forty days of restriction. Unfortunately, this would not be my last exposure to the side of the church that seemed to have forgotten the humanity it was intended to serve.[1]

Don't let it be lost on you that the Pharisees already knew the principles of justice, mercy, and faithfulness Jesus wanted them to get. They had scriptures about these very things committed to memory, scriptures like Proverbs 21:3: "To do what is right and just is more acceptable to the LORD than sacrifice." These religious leaders were also very familiar with the prophecies about the Messiah from one of their most respected prophets, Isaiah, that emphasized the same principles: "I will put my Spirit on him [the Messiah], and he will bring *justice* to the nations" (Isa. 42:1, emphasis added).

They were more than aware of the importance of these things to God, but they were distracted by gnats. This is the same problem Jesus addressed when he was asked the most ridiculous question of his ministry career. Jesus was teaching one day, and someone asked,

> "Teacher, which is the greatest commandment in the Law?"
>
> Jesus replied, "'Love the Lord your God.' . . . 'Love your neighbor as yourself.'" (Matt. 22:36–39)

I think the guy who asked the question quickly realized how dumb that question was, so he tried to redeem himself with a follow-up question, "Who is my neighbor?" (Luke 10:29), which was even worse.

I think he was a sports reporter.

The problem is, Jesus was the Son of God, and he knew this dude's heart. He knew he wasn't really this dumb. Perhaps Jesus knew this person's motive was to make sure that he only did what was required and not a bit more, that he was one of those gnat guys.

Let me sum up Jesus' response: "If you have to ask who your neighbor is, you're already a bad neighbor." You see, if you have to ask for a definition of *neighbor*, it really can't mean that you're hoping to do more. It can only mean that you're trying not to do any more than you *have* to do. There is no other way to interpret this question. Jesus knew what he was asking. He knew the one who stood before him was a *gracist*.

Like he did often, Jesus answered with a story. I'll summarize it for you. It's from Luke 10. Jesus said essentially,

> There's this guy. He was a Jewish guy. He was in Jerusalem on business, and he was on his way home. It's a seventeen-mile stretch of road to Jericho. It's not a good road, not a lot of highway patrol, not well lit, and a gang of thieves accosted him and beat him up and robbed him and left him for dead.
>
> But, never fear, because a priest, a church leader, happened to be going down the same road. If our poor, battered muggee had any consciousness left at all, if he could see out of either swollen eye, he probably thought, *Oh good. A holy man, a man of God, from my own religion, no less. This is going to be good for me.* But it wasn't, because the priest crossed the road and went around him.

This was Jesus' way of saying to the dumb-question guy, "I'm talking about you. Anybody who has to ask, 'Who is my neighbor?' is a bad neighbor. Let me describe a bad neighbor for you. It's a person who passes by on the other side to avoid being a neighbor at all."

Jesus continued,

> Somehow, on the priest's list of things to do, helping a battered man just didn't rank right up there. Maybe he didn't see the guy. Maybe he had church business to go to. He had

dill seeds to count and gnats to strain. Clueless about justice, mercy, and faithfulness, he was a camel-swallower.

Not to worry, along came a Levite. But alas, he also crossed the road and avoided being a neighbor.

You might ask yourself, *Why did the priest and the Levite cross the road?*

If you don't understand what a Levite was, let me tell you: he was an OCD neat freak for God. A Levite was a person who, on behalf of God, was in charge of making sure everybody followed the laws God had put in place. Many of the laws were about cleanliness, to protect them from germs and such. They were the ones who would offer sacrifices for the sins of the people who weren't clean.

One of the rules they had back in that day was not to touch dead people. That's a good rule, makes good sense to me. I see dead people . . . and I don't touch them. The problem for this Levite was that if he rolled this guy over and he was dead, he was going to be ceremonially unclean for seven days, which meant that he would not be able to go into the temple that weekend and do his church duties. Do you understand? This was a guy who thought God was more interested in his religious duties than he was in him loving his neighbor. I shudder to think how many needs we drive right by or walk right by on a daily basis. How many times do we not stop to help because we're on our way to church or to do church things?

Just like when the Pharisees confronted Jesus for healing a man on the Sabbath, saying, "Jesus, you broke the rule."

To which Jesus replied, "I healed him! What's more important?"

Remember, this is the exact type of church leader Jesus was telling this story to, those who strain gnats while swallowing camels.

Seeing People

Who is my neighbor? Literally the person you'd have to walk out of your way to avoid. That's the sarcastic wit in Jesus' story. The religious leaders went out of their way to avoid the injured man on the road. The area surrounding Jerusalem is very hilly, so if they were walking up or down a hill, it would have taken even more effort to avoid him. Yet, if you asked them later, they would probably have said, "I don't even know what you're talking about. I never saw that guy. What guy?"

Most of us, if we're honest, would agree with Donald Miller, CEO of StoryBrand, who said, "Billions of people live in the world, and somehow I can only muster thoughts for one. Me."[2]

In Jesus' story, he makes sure to point out that both church leaders saw the man yet walked by on the other side of the road. But did they really *see* him? Do you know what I'm asking? You can see but not see. How is it that if you can see a gnat in your wine and are able to count out your dill seeds, you can't see the crime scene by the side of the road?

I watched the Russell Crowe movie about Noah a few years ago on an international flight under the influence of Ambien, so take my critique with a grain of salt: it was really strange. I think there were angelic beings who looked like the Thing from *The Fantastic Four*. But the most bizarre scene was the ending, because Noah in this movie version had it in his head that God told him to build the ark not to save people but to judge humanity, and even to kill those who weren't chosen. There was this super tense and awkward moment where, after Noah's daughter-in-law delivered twin babies on the ark, Noah thought he was supposed to kill them.

In case you're wondering, this has nothing to do with the biblical narrative. It was even harder for me to process because the daughter-in-law is played by Emma Watson, Hermione from *Harry Potter*. I just couldn't get past it in the middle of the flight on this tiny screen, while the rest of the people on the plane were fast asleep.

So Noah, holding his knife, approached Hermione, who was holding her babies. Dumbledore was nowhere to be found. The orchestration built to a dramatic musical pause, while the violins reached a high point with extra reverberation. Nothing good was going to happen here. Then Noah *saw* the babies. He looked down into their eyes. And, at that moment, he realized he couldn't kill them. He loved them. Whew.

As bad a biblical translation as this movie was, that is the way Jesus tells us to *see*. We are to see the guy on the side of the road. See the people in need (especially if they are your grandchildren, Noah). See people through the lens of justice, mercy, and faithfulness. The priest and the Levite *looked* at the man; they didn't *see* him. All they saw were their rules and duty.

Notice the contrast between what the church leaders in this good Samaritan story did and how Jesus approached people in need:

> Jesus went through all the towns and villages, teaching in
> their synagogues, proclaiming the good news of the kingdom

and healing every disease and sickness. When he saw the crowds, he had compassion on them, because they were harassed and helpless, like sheep without a shepherd. (Matt. 9:35–36)

The difference is that Jesus saw people. I walk by people with messed-up lives many times, and sometimes I want to walk around them also. Often I'm just like the church leaders in this story. I skip right past the needs around me because I may have other things to do, or maybe I'm just a selfish jerk. What I do know is that I'm not seeing people through the lens of justice, mercy, and faithfulness. I don't see them as harassed and helpless like sheep without a shepherd. At that point, it doesn't really matter how many rules I follow or how well I do my religious duty.

Among the tribes of northern Natal in South Africa, the most common greeting, equivalent to "Hello" in English, is the expression *Sawubona*, which literally means "I see you." If you are a member of the tribe, you would reply by saying *Sikhona*, or "I am here." The order of the exchange is important: until you see me, I do not exist. It's as if when you see someone, you bring them into existence.

The church leaders in this story don't know what a neighbor is. But never fear; the hero of our story shows up, and he's a *Samaritan*! Doesn't that change the story for you? Jesus threw a giant curveball with the Samaritan protagonist. In Jewish storytelling, the third character is always the hero of the story. Just like in many of our jokes, where the third person is typically the fall guy or the punch line. This passage may actually be the origin of all of those jokes. "A priest, a rabbi, and Samaritan were walking down the road. . . ." Note that this would have caught the Jewish leaders' attention. Jesus set the scene of the story opposite of their expectations and then put their worst enemy at the heart of the story, as the hero. Of course, the "should we call down fire from heaven on them" disciples heard it too.

Jesus said, "But a certain Samaritan, as he journeyed, came to where he was. And *when he saw him*, he had compassion" (Luke 10:33 NKJV, emphasis added). There's a difference between seeing and *seeing*. The Samaritan had compassion when he saw the battered man. The Greek root word for *compassion* is *splanchnon*. This word describes a feeling that comes from the gut, which is exactly how it sounds when you say it. When you stop swallowing camels, you have room to feel empathy for the people you see.

What it means to be a compassionate neighbor is that when you see them with your gut, you feel what they're going through. It's not head knowledge, or even the heart; you just feel it in your inner being.

Jesus Twisted the Plot

What did the Samaritan do? He went to the broken man and bandaged his wounds, poured oil and wine over him, set him on his own animal, brought him to an inn, and took care of him, paying all his medical expenses.

A *good* Samaritan? The *hero* is a Samaritan? It's a plot twist. It's a clear illustration of the whole problem of gracism. It's a slap in the face to the Jewish leaders because, as we discussed with the woman at the well in chapter 8, the Jews and Samaritans didn't just not get along; there was a deep-rooted hatred between them. And truthfully, in the eyes of Jesus and anyone following the rules of God, these Samaritans were following an incorrect form of worship.

But remember that Jesus made up this story; it's not based on a factual occurrence. Why did he cast a Samaritan in this role? Because Jesus was telling us that it is possible for someone to have bad theology and still be a better neighbor than you. Their theology may lead them to swallow a few gnats, but at least the camels are safe. The real theology, the applied theology, is this: stop asking, "Who is my neighbor?" and start asking, "Won't you be my neighbor?"

It's not that theology (gnat straining) is unimportant. The problem occurs when we get so wrapped up in our theology that it doesn't affect us practically. If our vertical theology doesn't affect our horizontal vision, we can eventually become blinded. If we happen to be leading groups of other believers, this will make us into those "blind guides" Jesus referenced in Matthew 12.

> It is possible for someone to have bad theology and still be a better neighbor than you.

Then Jesus asked, "Which of these three do you think was neighbor to him who fell among the thieves?" (Luke 10:36 NKJV), and the dumb-question guy said, "He who showed mercy on him" (v. 37). Notice that he couldn't even bring himself to say, "the Samaritan." He said instead, "Uh, yeah, it was that third guy."

What Jesus says next is the most important part of the story: "Go and do likewise" (v. 37).

CHAPTER 11

WHEN OUR HEARTS GET IN THE WAY

Made a Difference to That One

"Then he will say to those on his left, 'Depart from me, you who are cursed, into the eternal fire prepared for the devil and his angels. For I was hungry and you gave me nothing to eat, I was thirsty and you gave me nothing to drink, I was a stranger and you did not invite me in, I needed clothes and you did not clothe me, I was sick and in prison and you did not look after me.'

"They also will answer, 'Lord, when did we see you hungry or thirsty or a stranger or needing clothes or sick or in prison, and did not help you?'

"He will reply, 'Truly I tell you, whatever you did not do for one of the least of these, you did not do for me.'"

(MATT. 25:41–45)

ONCE UPON A TIME, AS the story goes, there was an old man who would go to the ocean to do his writing. He had a habit of walking on the beach every morning before he began his work. Early one morning, he was walking along the shore after a big storm had passed and found the vast beach littered with starfish as far as the eye could see, stretching in both directions.

Off in the distance, the old man noticed a small boy walking, but as he walked, he would pause every so often. As the boy drew closer, the man saw that he was occasionally bending down to pick up an object and throw it into the sea. As the boy came closer still, the man called out, "Good morning! May I ask what it is that you're doing?"

The young boy paused, looked up, and replied, "Throwing starfish into the ocean. The tide has washed them up onto the beach, and they can't return to the sea by themselves. When the sun gets high, they will die, unless I throw them back into the water."

The old man replied, "But there must be tens of thousands of starfish on this beach. I'm afraid you won't really be able to make much of a difference."

The boy bent down, and picking up yet another starfish, threw it as far as he could into the ocean. Then he turned, smiled, and said, "It made a difference to that one!"[1]

As I have become involved in relief and justice and mission work in the developing world, I have learned a very important lesson: "making a difference to this one" is not the end-all answer to the problems of poverty and injustice in the world. As sweet as this starfish story is, we do need a bigger perspective and deeper answers.

So much of the time, we throw individual starfish back into the ocean without solving the problem of why they keep washing up on shore. Some of the reasons for that have to do with politics and corruption; some have to do with us, to borrow an expression, "giving out fish, instead of teaching them *how* to fish." I highly recommend a book called *When Helping Hurts* by Steve Corbett and Brian Fikkert for a better understanding of this complex dilemma.[2] This bigger picture is extremely valuable to keep in mind, but does that mean we forgo helping the one starfish in front of us?

Jesus was very clear that we do need to be personally involved in loving and saving and serving those who are in trouble around us. He goes so far as to say that we're not really even serving those who are "the least" when we do this, but actually serving Jesus himself: "[The King] will reply, 'Truly I tell you, whatever you did not do for one of the least of these, you did not do for me'" (Matt. 25:45).

It's mind-boggling, isn't it? This really messes with me. If I understand it correctly, that means that when I get off the interstate at my exit for home and there is a despondent-looking guy holding up a sad story written on cardboard about how he needs a handout for some reason, that's Jesus? What's more confusing is that I actually followed that guy one time back to his car that he had hidden down the road, and it didn't look like Jesus' car. It was nicer than mine!

I know there are many who are truly destitute and have no choice but to ask for handouts. But I've also talked to people who used to panhandle for a living, and they made more money doing that than most do at a real job. So how am I to know when to roll down my window and give? Should I just always do it? I mean, if the punishment for doing otherwise is God telling me to depart from him and into the devil's eternal fire, it seems I should err on the side of generosity.

Well, we're not going to heaven or hell based on our works, so I'll let you off the hook right up front. You're not going to get to the proverbial pearly gates, then find out that you missed a homeless person, so you can't get in. Nevertheless, when you consider Jesus' warnings about ignoring justice, and stories like the good Samaritan (Luke 10:25–37), not caring for the least of these is certainly something that made Jesus angry.

I've probably become too jaded in this area, to be honest. Sometimes the questions seem so big. Like, how do we reconcile what it means to care for the less fortunate? How do we solve the drastic problems of inequity in our world without enabling? This question has played a big part in shifting the emphasis for our church as we deal with the developing world. We have come to realize that much of our mission work has, in the long run, turned out to be unhealthy. What we were doing felt good to us at the time, and there have been some remarkable projects—it is always amazing to see how much can be done when we put people and resources in play—but in the long haul, our efforts haven't been very sustainable.

There is so much work to do. Four hundred million children around the world are living in extreme poverty, which is defined as living on less than $1.25 per day. Every day, 21,000 children die as a result of poverty or poverty-related preventable diseases. Every 3.6 seconds, a person dies of starvation, and most often it is a child under the age of five.[3]

What is our responsibility in the midst of this? The Bible is clear:

- John said, "For whoever does not love their brother and sister, whom they have seen, cannot love God, whom they have not seen" (1 John 4:20).

- Paul said, "[Godly people] share freely and give generously to the poor" (2 Cor. 9:9 NLT).
- Psalm 82:3–4 says, "Give justice to the poor and the orphan; uphold the rights of the oppressed and the destitute. Rescue the poor and helpless; deliver them from the grasp of evil people" (NLT).
- Jesus didn't mince words, either. He said, "[The King] will reply, 'Truly I tell you, whatever you did not do for one of the least of these, you did not do for me.' Then they will go away to eternal punishment, but the righteous to eternal life." (Matt. 25:45–46)

Philosopher Søren Kierkegaard described the tension so many of us feel between thought and action this way: "The Bible is very easy to understand—but we pretend to be unable to understand it, because we know very well that the minute we do, we are obligated to act accordingly."[4]

Someone Else Will Do It

Many times I have this conversation about our clear call to help the less fortunate and hear people say, "Yes! I agree. *We* need to do something." The problem is, there usually isn't much of "me" in that "we." Let's just be honest. It's really about someone else, their or our government or that nonprofit organization or those "rich people."

Like in the story of two small boys who walked into the dentist's office. One of them said bravely, "I want a tooth taken out, and I don't want any gas. And I don't want it deadened . . . because we're in a hurry!"

The dentist said, "You're quite a brave young man. Which tooth is it?"

The boy turned to his smaller friend and said, "Show him your tooth, Albert."

Listen again to the words of Jesus: "[The King] will reply, 'Truly I tell you, whatever you did not do for one of the least of these, you did not do for me'" (Matt. 25:45). It is the same thing he said on the positive side (v. 40): "Whatever you did for one of the least of these . . . you did for me." It's not about *them*; it's about *you*. It's not about *we*; it's about *me*.

Why am I so convinced? Because Jesus is always concerned with the root of all problems, which is our hearts. His longest recorded teaching in the Gospels, which we refer to as the Sermon on the Mount (Matt. 5–7), was all about the heart. There, Jesus told us that hate is the same as murder because of our hearts. Lust is the same as adultery because of our hearts. Essentially, the heart is the heart of the matter.

It's not about *we*; it's about *me*.

In the Matthew 25 passage about the poor, hungry, and imprisoned, Jesus was angry at *both* the act of ignoring the "least" *and* the fact that our hearts were so hard that we didn't even realize there was a need: "When did we see you hungry or thirsty or a stranger or needing clothes or sick or in prison . . . ?" (v. 44).

If that person I serve, the "least of these," is really Jesus, then wasn't he trying to show us that visiting, giving, feeding, and clothing the less fortunate might just as much be for *our benefit* as for theirs? What we're missing is a very important cardiac therapy for our own souls.

As I've hinted, there is a big debate in social justice circles about taking people from the *developed* world on short-term trips to help in the *developing* world. For good reason. I'm closely connected enough on both sides to more fully understand the issue. Honestly, it is rarely cost effective to the receiving organization in terms of time and energy when a group from a developed world comes to help. It is also, as I've already stated, counterproductive to provide fish instead of teaching how to fish. Yet we still do it, and I recommend you do it too. I know that *my life* has been changed by going to other places to serve Jesus.

I met Jesus on my first trip to Nairobi. His name was Collins Otiendo. He lived with his family in the Mathare district of Nairobi, Kenya, a part of town the Kenyan government didn't even want to acknowledge existed at that time. I've seen poverty in many parts of the world, but nothing compared to the tin villages of Nairobi. I carefully navigated as I walked into Mathare, so as not to step in the wastewater canal that ran between the rows of shacks. The district had no electricity, running water, or bathrooms. I was warned to avoid any plastic bags that might be lying on the ground. Those bags were known as "flying toilets," which described the practice of people relieving themselves into the bags and throwing them out the window.

Many of the children looked at me with great surprise and shock, having never seen a white man before. I'm usually great with babies, but, well, think about kids sitting on Santa's lap at the mall. I might as well have been dressed like a scary clown.

On that first visit, which is forever etched in my memory as one of my life-changing moments, I met the Otiendo family.

The father was gone, the mother had HIV/AIDS, and the rest of the family lived in a tin-walled room with no facilities of any kind. There wasn't even any light, which creates exactly the kind of dangerous territory you would imagine when the sun goes down. The younger kids were being cared for by the ministry I was there to visit, Missions of Hope International (MOHI), which had a child sponsorship program. But Collins, the young man who changed my life with his big, goofy Jesus smile, was graduating from the program, along with his older brother, George. They would soon be stuck living on the streets because high school sponsorship was not available.

I couldn't let that happen, so I got involved with Collins, the starfish, and his family. Our church helped MOHI start a sponsorship program for older kids. And, with the help of one of my friends, I unofficially adopted Collins and George. I was able to visit them and the ministry several times, as well as with my entire family. One of my daughters spent a summer working in the program in Nairobi. In time, Collins became part of our family; he called me Dad, and I called him Son. My friends and I also helped finance a home and property for his family. The boys graduated from high school and college with education degrees, and Collins had plans to start his own school.

Along the way, our church became more heavily involved in child sponsorships and provided an efficient way to help people make a difference. Now many churches in the United States work together to provide tens of thousands of children with food, education, and the love of God at sixteen schools around Kenya. Many local churches are also involved in the program and have become part of the solution to helping the "least of these."

But don't let this sound like a poverty success story. That's not my point. Well, I guess it is, but the poverty was *mine*, not Collins's. My last email from Collins was two weeks before he died. It turns out he had an undetected enlarged heart, and it just stopped one day. Sadly, in many ways, Collins was still a casualty of poverty. His heart condition could have been caused by an infection at a young age, or it might have been genetic. But with no health care or family history, there was no detection until it was too late. If he had grown up in a place with regular health care, it's likely that his problem would have been discovered and treated.

Collins is with Jesus now. It's still a painful reality for me, but as I look back, I'm able to see Matthew 25 from a different angle. What if the sheep-goat judgment from Jesus was not about how many starfish we throw back, but about whether we even see them in the first place?

My Hard Heart

Scholars have debated Matthew 25:41–43 ad nauseum, because at face value it seems to offer a works-oriented salvation. Like heaven is for the good people and hell is for the bad ones. Honestly, it's never been that difficult for me. As Paul told us in Romans, "We maintain that a person is justified by faith apart from the works of the law" (Rom. 3:28). Salvation by grace is the paramount reason Jesus came and died; he did it for all my sins, including my hard heart. When the thief on the cross asked to go into the kingdom, Jesus didn't say, "Well, sure, as soon as you go work at a soup kitchen for a few days."

History's best guess is that the writer of another letter in the New Testament, named James, was the brother of Jesus. (No pressure there.) Let's look at what he had to say about this:

> What good is it, my brothers and sisters, if someone claims to have faith but has no deeds? Can such faith save them? Suppose a brother or a sister is without clothes and daily food. If one of you says to them, "Go in peace; keep warm and well fed," but does nothing about their physical needs, what good is it? In the same way, faith by itself, if it is not accompanied by action, is dead.
>
> But someone will say, "You have faith; I have deeds."
>
> Show me your faith without deeds, and I will show you my faith by my deeds. (James 2:14–18)

It's possible to have a head knowledge of God, and even follow the literal rules of God, without ever having a heart transplant. But the essence of the Gospels is heart transformation. What James was saying is that it takes more than belief to follow Jesus. Look at James 2:19: "You believe that there is one God. Good! Even the demons believe that—and shudder." It's not about belief; it's about your heart. Tim Keller says it this way: "The verdict leads to performance. It is not the performance that leads to the verdict."[5]

Jesus was teaching a crowd of people who thought they were connected to God, but their hearts hadn't made the transition yet. This is why we need to personally connect with the "least of these." Because they *are* Jesus for us. Collins was Jesus to me. I was the one who learned from Jesus in that relationship, although Collins probably would have disagreed.

Experts would tell you that without my compassion to throw that starfish back into the sea, Collins would have dried up in the sun, or he might not have survived as long as he did, or worse yet, he might have become part of the problem instead of the solution on that uncontrolled stretch of beach where so many starfish perish. But the impact this relationship had on me, my family, and my heart is worth far more to me and him than any food, education, or roof to sleep under. I'm sure he would agree with that.

Our daughter Lauren spent six months in Bolivia in a safe house for girls while she was attending Wheaton College. Bolivia is one of the poorest countries in Latin America, and these were the least-of-these girls in a least-of-these country. She smiled as she told us the story about one of the girls in the safe house, Betty, who had come from the jungle, and from a very bad situation. Betty had never heard about Jesus. But one day, when Lauren walked into her room and saw her drawing, she asked, "Who are you drawing a picture of?"

Betty said, "Jesus."

Lauren had to bite her lip to keep from laughing. In the drawing, Jesus had curly hair and really pretty eyes, and he looked like a woman.

Betty knew Jesus was a man, but Lauren said it dawned on her that the only people who had ever been Jesus to her were female. She drew a feminine Jesus because women were the witnesses in her life.

This is what Jesus was talking about in Matthew 25. As we build relationships with and serve the people we are called to see, Jesus is revealed. Collins and I became Jesus to each other, and when we did, both of our worlds improved.

So, what should we do when we're unsure about how to move forward against the backdrop of bigger questions like how to better address poverty and injustice? We should certainly think about making sure that the help we offer does more good than harm, but you can throw out that cost-benefit analysis when it comes to relationships.

I know that our relationship itself meant more to Collins than anything else. The last time I physically saw him and George was when I had a layover in Nairobi on my way to Malawi, and they made drastic arrangements to come by and surprise me in that small window of time. They were just giddy—that's the only word I can think of—which is so un-Kenyan, being that Kenyans are a very reserved people. My last memory of Collins is a video we made singing "Happy Birthday" to my daughter (their sister) Becca, as we parted company that day. I play the video regularly when I think about how much I miss him. "Happy Birthday, dear Beeekah."

It's easy to be overcome with a sense of helplessness when we consider issues such as poverty and hunger and injustice in the world. I can't fix it for everyone. I'm just one person. But it is important that I fix it for someone. I would venture to say that everyone knows someone who could use a little help. Everyone knows someone who is lonely, sick, poor, or imprisoned in some way. And by the way, George and the family are doing well, and I'm still involved.

For those of us feeling that weight while looking at the enormity of the situation, I'd suggest going back to Luke 9:12–13. Jesus was in Bethsaida, speaking to the multitudes who had gathered to hear him:

Late in the afternoon the Twelve came to him and said, "Send the crowd away so they can to the surrounding villages and countryside and find food and lodging, because we are in a remote place here."

He replied, "You give them something to eat."

The disciples' response to the needs they saw was, "There are just too many needs here, Jesus."

But Jesus told them, "You give them something to eat."

Seeing that they were overwhelmed, he then asked, "Let's do what we can with what we have. What do you have?" (Now, that is a good question. What do you have?) Jesus said, "You do it. You give them something to eat. Quit playing church and start doing justice and mercy and faithfulness."

"Well, what should I do?"

"What do you have?"

Bob Goff says it so well, "Don't make this more complicated than it is. Just start. Go find someone who is hungry right now and do something about it. I've heard lots of people say that giving the poor a fishing pole is better than giving them a meal, but I don't see them giving away many fish or poles."[6]

This is obviously not a small issue to Jesus. And it may be that it's not even as much about the person you're helping as it is about you. What if the "made a difference to that one" is about you, and not the starfish?

And what if that one is your neighbor or your friend or even a little child?

141

CHAPTER 12

WHEN LITTLE CHILDREN GET IN THE WAY

Say Hello to My Little Friend

"If anyone causes one of these little ones—those who believe in me—to stumble, it would be better for them to have a large millstone hung around their neck and to be drowned in the depths of the sea."

(MATT. 18:6)

EVERY OLDER GENERATION THINKS THE younger ones have it easier. That's just natural because it's true. Humanity is good at innovation, and life does get easier in many ways. It doesn't matter how old you are; just think of how things have changed. It's possible that my grandchildren will never learn to drive because transportation will be automated. It's amazing how things change.

When I was a kid there was no internet. If you wanted to know something, you had to go to the library and look it up. There was no social media, email, texting, or messaging. If you wanted to talk to a girl, you had to pass a note through three of her friends. I guess that's about as gutless as texting now that I think about it. Some things never change.

There was no way to record TV shows either. If you wanted to watch *The Wizard of Oz*, you had to watch it when it was on, with commercials. It seemed to always be on during Sunday night when my parents made me go to church, so I was an adult before I realized Dorothy was trying to get back to Kansas. (Which still makes no sense to me.)

Back then there were only three or four channels on TV, and you had to use a little book called *TV Guide* to find out what was on when (that is, if your parents weren't as cheap as mine and bought you one). And the cartoons were only on Saturday mornings, so you couldn't sleep in. There were no virtual-reality video games with high-resolution graphics. We had Pong. Look it up.

The world is a different place today and changing every minute. Now try to imagine people from Jesus' day walking around in the twenty-first century. They would be fascinated by many things. I'm sure technology would be the most surprising. But the sociology would also blow them away. As many social problems as we still have in regard to how we treat each other, people from the first century would marvel at how well we all—races and tribes—get along, seeing the near elimination of slavery and the major strides with regard to equality of women. And they would be absolutely fascinated by the way we treat our children, the care and protection we give.

I don't mean to suggest that people of old didn't love their children, but they cared for them very differently. It makes me laugh to think about one of those people trying to open a child-proof handle or put a child in a car seat. As with technology, we've come a long way, even in my lifetime, regarding how we take care of our children. Back in my day we didn't have nets around the trampoline. We just fell off. Back in my day we didn't have seat belts. We just slid back and forth on the vinyl, hanging on for dear life. And sometimes I slept in the back window. Okay, I'll stop.

I don't know what they'd think about the way we care for children, but I know I'm grateful, because I love children, and so did Jesus. One of the angry incidents of Jesus in the Bible came about when the disciples didn't value children enough. Mark 10:14 even tells us that Jesus "was indignant" in response to the situation. Indignant means "to have a strong feeling of displeasure and antagonism as the result of some real or supposed wrong—'to be very angry, to be full of anger.'"[1]

Why was Jesus indignant? This situation started days earlier, in another funny story.

The Story Started Days Earlier . . .

According to Mark 9:34, it all began with a "discussion" the disciples were having about who was going to be the greatest in the kingdom. I don't care how long you follow Jesus, selfishness is going to continue to creep into your soul.

What's great about this story is that for some reason, James and John's mother got involved. Their mom asked Jesus if her sons could sit next to him on the throne (Matt. 20:20–21). Can you picture it? Hey, James and John, what is your mom doing here? I guess I need to have an endorsement for this book from my mom, now that I think about it.

Matthew 20:24 records that after this happened, the other

ten became "indignant" toward the two of them. We must remember that most of the disciples were young at the time, but this is still a bizarre story. This was more than simply calling shotgun. They were positioning for power. What I'd like to know is whether the other ten were indignant because of what James, John, and their mom were trying to pull, or because they hadn't thought of it first. Regardless, we know there was tension. Jesus knew there was tension.

> They came to Capernaum. When he was in the house, he
> asked them, "What were you arguing about on the road?"
> But they kept quiet because on the way they had argued about
> who was the greatest. (Mark 9:33–34)

If I may paraphrase, Jesus asked, "So what were you two arguing about back there?"

"Oh, nothing."

Jesus was just messing with them. He obviously knew what their argument was about, so he decided to set the record straight. "You guys keep forgetting that I'm Jesus, and I can hear you. I heard your little quarrel. Here is your answer about who gets to ride up front in the kingdom of God."

Remember that Jesus' goal was for these disciples not just to *ride* in the kingdom, but to *drive* it. Jesus was going to leave the keys to the kingdom bus to them (Matt. 16:19), so they had to get this right! It always amazes me that Jesus has entrusted a small part of his kingdom to the likes of leaders like me. I guess I don't know for sure that he actually has, but I've been leading one of his churches for almost thirty years now and haven't been struck by lightning yet, so allow me my delusion.

In this twenty-first century, I'm just one of the tiny, insignificant specks of leadership in his gigantic and eternal kingdom, so there is a limit to what I can screw up. But these disciples were different. They were the Twelve! These guys were the make-or-break leadership team that was going to start the church. If they failed, Jesus would have died in vain. Yet here they were, shoving to get in front of each other in line! No wonder Jesus seemed a bit testy.

Jesus called a child over and had him stand in their midst. They were in Peter's town, and some scholars speculate that the child might have been someone from Peter's family. The majority of my parishioners grew up with priests who couldn't marry, and it usually surprises them to learn that Peter—Pope Numero Uno in their world—was married. We know this because Jesus healed Peter's mother-in-law in Matthew 8:14. No one has a mother-in-law just for the heck of it.

But I digress. There was a kid there, and Jesus used this child as an illustration. He said, "I tell you the truth, unless you turn from your sins and become like little children, you will never get into the Kingdom of Heaven" (Matt. 18:3 NLT). He could have added, "much less *lead* the kingdom of heaven!"

Jesus continued, "Whoever humbles himself like this child is the greatest in the kingdom of heaven" (Matt. 18:4 ESV).

All eyes turned to this child Jesus called over. Kids can become the center of attention very quickly if called upon. This reminds me of a story of a woman and a child in a church service. One day, as the pastor started his prayer, "Dear Lord, without you, we are but dust . . . ," her daughter leaned over to ask quite audibly in her shrill little-girl voice, "Mom, what is 'but dust'?"

I'd still rather be with kids than grown-ups. Adults are boring. They have adult things to get done, important items to conquer, seats of honor to fight for in the kingdom. I agree with Jesus: kids are better.

Jesus said also, "And whoever welcomes one such child in my name welcomes me" (Matt. 18:5). If this sounds familiar, it should. In chapter 11, Jesus taught us that when we do for the "least of these," we've done it for him. Greatness is about loving the least, not excluding them.

Mark takes it even a step further: "Anyone who welcomes a little child like this on my behalf welcomes me, and anyone who welcomes me welcomes not only me but also my Father who sent me" (Mark 9:37 NLT). Welcoming children means welcoming Jesus. Welcoming Jesus means welcoming God. In the same way, my son Collins was Jesus to me. Jesus is the "least," and our ministry to "the least"—no matter their age, gender, race, incarceration status, or economic status—changes us. It affects our gut (*splanchnon*), our eyes, and ultimately our hearts.

It is hard for us to imagine how much less children were respected in Jesus' day. The early church became known as a community that cared for children in a rare, special way, because they did a beautiful job of understanding what Jesus taught here.

Aristides told the Roman emperor Hadrian about first-century Christians in this way:

> They love one another. They never fail to help widows; they save orphans from those who would hurt them. If they have something they give freely to the man who has nothing; if they see a stranger, they take him home, and are happy, as though he were a real brother. They don't consider themselves brothers in the usual sense, but brothers instead through the Spirit, in God.[2]

Obviously, they had learned from Jesus' anger. Hopefully, we will as well.

John Ortberg gives us more background on the impact of Jesus' attitude toward children in his excellent book, *Who Is This Man?* He points out how great the contrast was between "Herod, the Great" and "Jesus, the child":

> A new time had come with Jesus, a time when thinking about kings and children would begin to shift. You might say there was an idea lying there in the manger along with a baby. An idea that had mostly been confined to a little country called Israel, but which was waiting for the right time to crawl out into the wider world—an idea which that wider world would be unable to wholly resist.
>
> All peoples in the ancient world had gods. Their gods had different names, but what they shared was a hierarchical way of ordering life. At the top of creation were the gods; under them was the king. Under the king were members of the court and the priests, who reported to the king. Below them were artisans, merchants, and craftspeople, and below them was a large group of peasants and slaves—the dregs of humanity. . . .
>
> This is the Dignity Gap. The farther down the ladder, the wider the gap. But that gap was challenged by an idea that lay there in the manger, an idea that had been guarded by Israel for centuries: There is one God. He is good. And every human being has been made in his image.[3]

Charles Dickens also wrote in *A Christmas Carol*, "It is good to be children sometimes, and never better than Christmas, when its mighty Founder was a child Himself."[4]

When the Messiah came in the form of a baby, that changed the whole scorecard for what it meant to be great, especially when we consider that the baby was humbled to the point of execution on a cross (Phil. 2:5–11).

One of the Craziest Things He Said

All this is the background for one of the craziest things Jesus ever said. It's so bizarre and out of character that it has to be very important. The gospel writers could not have misheard this:

> "If anyone causes one of these little ones—those who believe in me—to stumble, it would be better for them to have a large millstone hung around their neck and to be drowned in the depths of the sea." (Matt. 18:6)

Huh? Did Jesus really say that? I can't hear this phrase coming from Jesus' mouth without a mushy Italian accent, can you? Like "You will sleep with the fishes," or "Say hello to my little friend."

Let me clarify, just in case you think maybe this is one of those interpretation issues, like maybe Jesus' millstone might have been some kind of a fancy jewel you could put in a nice necklace. A millstone was so heavy that you needed an animal to move it with a lever. You heard it right the first time. This was yet another horrible form of capital punishment in the days of old. Jesus' audience would have heard this exactly as "the electric chair would be better for you." Jesus is not threatening to electrocute you; he's just saying it would be better if someone did. It's that serious.

150

The millstone warning above is in Matthew as well as Mark 9:42 and Luke 17:2. So you know it made a huge impression on the disciples. It was not a statement that would have been easy to forget coming from anyone, let alone the Rabbi who said the greatest commandments were about love and turning the other cheek and praying for our enemies! This was a mic-drop moment. I imagine the disciples turning to each other and giving that quizzical look, like, "What'd he say?" It gets better.

Mark reports that just a few days later, "People were bringing little children to Jesus for him to place his hands on them, but the disciples rebuked them. When Jesus saw this, he was indignant" (Mark 10:13–14). Mad!

Considering this background information, I believe Jesus was yelling this next verse: "Let the little children come to me, and do not hinder them, for the kingdom of God belongs to such as these" (Mark 10:14). I had always imagined this statement being uttered in that voice you use when trying to get a puppy not to be afraid of you. I pictured Jesus squatting down to encourage the kids to come, saying in this higher-pitched voice, "It's okay, Peter and John. Let them through. Awww. Come on over here, kids. It's okay."

With the fuller perspective we've just discussed, though, this changes the scene. I think he was yelling! I'm surprised the kids didn't all run and hide. I believe "Let the children come to me" was leveled at the disciples, as in "What part of 'when you welcome children, you welcome me,' did you not understand?! Don't make me go get my millstone!"

This was one of the few times Jesus was angry with his own team; usually he was angry at the church leaders of his day. It all comes down to the same core issue: denied access to the love of the Father. This makes Jesus mad (indignant).

I'm certain the disciples had good intentions. To be fair, children weren't allowed to become students of a rabbi until a certain age, and the text seems to make the distinction that these kids weren't old enough for school. So it makes sense that the disciples assumed Jesus would be wasting his time being with them. They also knew how much of a distraction kids could be, and that Jesus was in the middle of an important teaching moment.

Side note: It's possible that Jesus had ADHD. Go read the Sermon on the Mount. He goes, "Here is how you should pray. And give this way. And don't worry about stuff. Did someone mention divorce? Well, the gate is narrow." I mean, Jesus was all over the place!

What were we talking about? Oh yeah, distractions: the children. Jesus was teaching the important grown-up people, and the disciples didn't want the little people getting in the way. That's when Jesus got mad. To make his point as strongly as possible, he even brought in supernatural reinforcements: "See that you do not despise one of these little ones. For I tell you that their angels in heaven always see the face of my Father in heaven" (Matt. 18:10).

He was saying that there is something very special about children, that the angels in heaven don't see them (children) but the face of God. He already told us that when we welcome them, we welcome God (Mark 9:37). When we add it to his statement in Matthew 25:40 about the "least of these brothers and sisters of mine," it's safe to say that Jesus most readily identified himself with those who couldn't take care of themselves.

In my first book, *Life on Mission*, I took this scripture about tying big rocks around your neck and throwing you into the sea, to point out how much more we need to do to take care of the children of the world, and we do. Children should not be hungry, sick, or hurt in any way. I'm glad for trampoline nets. I want to put one around all the children of the world. But the phrase Jesus used when he said not to hinder them, usually translates to "cause to sin." This goes even deeper than whether they have food or a place to sleep. The Greek word for *hinder* is *skandalizó*, which means "to put a snare (in the way), hence to cause to stumble, to give offense."

Pope Benedict used this passage correctly when he used it to confront the heinous acts of violence and abuse against children, especially by those charged with their spiritual care. Let me tell you, I think child abusers of any kind need to be punished to the fullest extent, and they should never be allowed to have the opportunity to do it again. I know the expression, "Hurt people hurt people," and these abusers were likely abused in some way themselves in the past. But someone has to stop the cycle.

However, it's the deeper issue of a child's soul that Jesus was really talking about here. This "causing to sin" is not just about whether these children are naked, hungry, or sick. It's not even about what horrible people do to children's bodies. This is about the eternal souls of children. I don't know about you, but I'm thinking that if this issue is a hot button for Jesus, we should look at it from a deeper perspective. What are we doing to encourage children to connect with their heavenly Father? We must be careful not to do anything that would damage a child's faith in a trustworthy God by being an untrustworthy guardian. Be mindful not to be the person who gives a child cause for cynicism.

Jesus views a child's innocent faith as something wholly valid and worth protecting. So we need to do everything we can to help the next generation on their journey of faith. Of course, we need to feed and clothe and educate them, but we cannot be cavalier about their faith. Honestly, it's one of the reasons I'm writing this book. We, the church, have to get this right! We have to make sure we're not blocking their access to Jesus, and therefore access to God. Nothing is more important. Jesus said we would be better off with a big rock tied around our necks and thrown into the sea if we ever got in their way.

Can I just point out to you once again the verse we should all take to heart? "Let the little children come to me, and do not hinder them, for the kingdom of God belongs to such as these" (Mark 10:14).

When Does Belief Begin?

Jesus said, "Your Father in heaven is not willing that any of these little ones should perish" (Matt. 18:14). So, I've got questions. When is a person old enough to have faith in God? How does it begin? How early could we be in danger of the wrath of Jesus for blocking access to children?

I know that every children's ministry director who finds out about this book is going to buy at least one copy. The stats tell you a vast majority of people who decide to follow Jesus do it before age eighteen, so I can't really imagine how you take that stat, mix it with a side of millstone, and not do killer children's ministry. No brainer. Give a copy of this book to your pastor with a bookmark on this chapter and say, "I'm going to make you an offer you can't refuse."

But there is a deeper level of conversation we need to have on this subject. If you're like me, you've probably assumed along the way, somewhere in your subconscious, that faith is something you're capable of possessing as you get closer to adulthood. If you've dug into some hard theology at any point in your faith journey, or you've come up against questions you couldn't answer, or walked through dark seasons and wrestled with God, you might look at a child and think, *They couldn't possibly grasp this stuff!*

And, of course, you'd be right. Which is also part of Jesus' point. Does Jesus tell us that kids should be more like adults? No. He said, "Whoever humbles himself like this child is the greatest in the kingdom of heaven" (Matt. 18:4 ESV). Oh. Elementary students probably aren't going to be arguing about eschatology (end times) anytime soon. I think Jesus knew our adult tendency to get deeply distracted from the main point and was directing us back to the simpler faith of childhood.

Listen, learn all you can. I'm glad you picked up this book. I hope it deepens your love for Jesus. I also hope you pick up many more books along the way. Yes, learn all you can. Just don't get distracted from the crux of the good news, which is that God loves you so much he died for you! He loves your neighbor who believes differently about predestination than you do too. He loves your coworker who voted differently from you as well. He loves that other person of another race, another denomination, another generation, fill in the blank. And you know what's crazy? Kids get that. They get it better than we grown-ups do. As Jesus said, "Truly I tell you, unless you change and become like little children, you will never enter the kingdom of heaven" (Matt. 18:3).

Jesus is not only discrediting the idea that kids don't understand God and faith, he is actually telling us that children get God better than the adults, and "unless we change and become like little children," *we will never enter the kingdom.*

The Questions We Wrestle with . . . and Kids Don't

There are many implications in this instance of Jesus' anger, his radical sweeping statements about the kingdom and our faith, and what the whole thing ought to look like. But I don't believe this is an affront to deeper theology.

As we age and grow in maturity, wrestling through hard questions and dark seasons, hopefully we will develop a deeper love for God and clearer understanding of his character. But let's never think ourselves too knowledgeable that we lose that original, innocent trust. Let's not buy into the world's lie that cynicism is wisdom. Let's not get caught up in climbing that tower and forget we don't have to ascend to God, because Jesus came down to us.

My friend Casey Tygrett talks about the practice of asking questions to avoid becoming cynical in his book, *Becoming Curious.* Kids ask around four hundred questions a day because they know that they don't know. They're trying to figure out their world. But we slowly lose this curiosity throughout our lives as we're taught that asking questions shows that we don't have it all together.

156

We're in bad shape when we start thinking we have it all together, like the church leaders did. I poked fun at the end-times theology earlier; it is one of my great frustrations with grown-up Christians. So many people spend so much time trying to figure out something Jesus assured us we would never figure out. He said even he didn't know when it was going to happen while he was with us (Mark 13:32). It's important to understand how our story ends, but so many people are, well, straining gnats and swallowing camels with eschatology.

But let's return to it for a minute. It might help us better understand the "unless you change and become like little children" warning from Jesus.

> Let's not get caught up in climbing that tower and forget we don't have to ascend to God, because Jesus came down to us.

Kids might be the only people really poised to have the correct view of Revelation: Jesus rides on this flying horse, and there's a huge battle, but then he slays the dragon with his sword and the good guys win! Right? There it is. Done.

Neil Gaiman, in his book *Coraline*, paraphrases G. K. Chesterton this way: "Fairy tales are more than true; not because they tell us that dragons exist, but because they tell us that dragons can be beaten."[5] Every kid knows a story is supposed to have a happy ending. Why? Why do kids love fairy tales so much? Because God wrote it on our hearts. We are born knowing that our Prince really will come, that there will be a glorious wedding someday, and that the dragon will be slain. But somewhere along the way, we convinced ourselves that it was too good to be true. Life beat us down, and we forgot how to hope for a happy ending. That is, until Jesus came and reminded us. The kids actually have it right.

I love Eugene Peterson's translation of Colossians 1:28: "We teach in a spirit of profound common sense so that we can bring each person to maturity. To be mature is to be basic. Christ! No more, no less" (THE MESSAGE). If we're going to take Paul at his word here, we should argue less about which current world leader might be the Antichrist and spend more time loving others and being curious.

Up to this point, I've been pretty critical of the church. I hope you don't misunderstand my intention. I believe we have the greatest opportunity to advance the kingdom through the church today than we have ever had. We are poised for impact if we get this right. I believe Jesus loves how far we've come and so much of what is being done in his name in the world today.

If we are interpreting Jesus' millstone comment, and his indignation at blocking access to the "least of these," whether it be the children, the naked, the hungry, or the sick, let me share a story that puts it all on the table in a good way. It's a football story, in Texas. If you don't understand the significance of that introduction, ask someone. Football is a god, with a little *g*, in some states, of which Texas is one. This is a story about taking Jesus seriously in regard to everything we've been talking about over the last few chapters. Let's begin.[6]

Grapevine Faith Baptist is a private Christian prep school. One year they made an arrangement to play football against Gainesville State School, a correctional facility for juvenile offenders. Kris Hogan, coach of the Faith team, had a radical Jesus idea about how to let the students come to Jesus. Faith always had a good football program; they were 7–2 going into the game. They also had money, equipment, coaches, and supportive parents. Gainesville was 0–8. Working at a correctional facility is not a dream job for coaches. They also had few resources and kids who came and went depending on their conviction sentencing. And truthfully, it's not likely that many of these kids had supportive parents in the stands.

Coach Hogan and his crew set up his plan with their families and the football fans ahead of time. He asked half of the attendees to go to the other side and cheer for the other team for this one night. He wrote to the fans:

> Here's the message I want you to send: you are just as valuable as any other person on planet Earth.

When one of his players asked why they were doing this, he said,

> Imagine if you didn't have a home life. Imagine if everybody had pretty much given up on you. Now imagine what it would mean for hundreds of people to suddenly believe in you.

It started with half of the Faith fans making a spirit line for their opponents to run through while they cheered them on, complete with a big banner for them to crash through at the end with their team name on it. These fans really got into it. They knew their names and everything.

"I never in my life thought I'd hear people cheering for us to hit their kids," recalls Isaiah, Gainesville's quarterback.

"I thought maybe they were confused," said Alex, a Gainesville lineman. "They started yelling, 'DEE-fense!' when their team had the ball. I said, 'What? Why are they cheerin' for us?'"

"We can tell people are a little afraid of us when we come to the games," says Gerald, a lineman with a three-year sentence. "You can see it in their eyes. They're lookin' at us like we're criminals. But these people, they were yellin' for us! By our names!"

As expected, the Lions still won the game handily. Texas coaches can be nice, but not nice enough to actually *lose* a game. Even so, the Gainesville kids were so happy that they gave *their* head coach, Mark Williams, a Gatorade shower anyway.

After the game, both Faith and Gainesville gathered in the field to pray. This seems like it would have made Jesus very happy. Isaiah from Gainesville surprised everybody when he volunteered to lead the prayer. Coach Hogan recalled that no one had any idea what he was going to say. Isaiah prayed, "Lord, I don't know how this happened, so I don't know how to say thank You. But I never would've known there was so many people in the world that cared about us."

The reporter covering this for ESPN said, "And it was a good thing everybody's heads were bowed because they might've seen Hogan wiping away tears."

As the young men walked back to their bus escorted by guards, the community from Faith met each of them with a bag for the ride home that contained some snacks, a Bible, and a personal encouraging letter from a Faith player. When Coach Williams got a moment with Coach Hogan later, he grabbed his shoulders and said, "You'll never know what your people did for these kids tonight. You'll never, ever know."

Jesus knew. And he told it to his disciples over two thousand years ago.

CHAPTER 13

WHEN JOYLESS, SELFISH PEOPLE GET IN THE WAY

Old Dogs, Old Tricks

"Meanwhile, the older son was in the field."

(LUKE 15:25)

I QUALIFY FOR THE SENIOR discount at IHOP. I've been getting AARP applications in the mail for a long time. I'm a grandpa times five (one on the way), and proud of it. I'm dedicating this book to my grandchildren. I hope their generation understands Jesus better than any of us today.

There are some advantages to being older. Weddings and colleges are paid for. I have more wisdom. Grandchildren are crazy cool. But there are some disadvantages as well. Aches and pains. Middle-of-the-night trips to the bathroom. The need for a nose-hair trimmer.

I love the story of the two older gentlemen who are talking about restaurants one day while their wives are in another room.

One of them says, "We ate at the best place last week. I can't think of the name of it. What's the name of that flower that smells nice and looks nice and has prickly thorns?"

The other guy says, "You mean a rose?"

The first man says, "Yeah, that's it." Then he yells into the other room, "Rose, what's the name of that restaurant we ate at last week?"

As we age, not only do we lose our memory and hair and control of our functions, but we also become set in our ways. The old adage, "You can't teach an old dog new tricks," is really not about the capabilities of the dog but the attitude of the dog. Once an old dog gets set in its ways, it's hard for it to learn new patterns. I'm really glad this isn't true for humans.

The parable of the prodigal son is fascinating to me. We usually call it by that name, probably because we can all relate to the prodigal, wayward son. I certainly do. However, the seemingly bad boy is not the truly bad boy in this story. The real bad boy is the prodigal son's older brother. But Jesus used the example of the prodigal son's rebellion as a way to shock his audience with the grace of an amazing Father. This story is really about the Father, not the son. It's really about God and his love for his children.

Jesus told this story in response to the Pharisees' grumbling:

> Now the tax collectors and sinners were all drawing near to hear him. And the Pharisees and the scribes grumbled, saying, "This man receives sinners and eats with them." (Luke 15:1–2 ESV)

Actually, he told them three stories. But this one was the clincher:

And he said, "There was a man who had two sons. And the younger of them said to his father, 'Father, give me the share of property that is coming to me.' And he divided his property between them. Not many days later, the younger son gathered all he had and took a journey into a far country, and there he squandered his property in reckless living. And when he had spent everything, a severe famine arose in that country, and he began to be in need. So he went and hired himself out to one of the citizens of that country, who sent him into his fields to feed pigs. And he was longing to be fed with the pods that the pigs ate, and no one gave him anything.

"But when he came to himself, he said, 'How many of my father's hired servants have more than enough bread, but I perish here with hunger! I will arise and go to my father, and I will say to him, "Father, I have sinned against heaven and before you. I am no longer worthy to be called your son. Treat me as one of your hired servants."' And he arose and came to his father. But while he was still a long way off, his father saw him and felt compassion, and ran and embraced him and kissed him. And the son said to him, 'Father, I have sinned against heaven and before you. I am no longer worthy to be called your son.' But the father said to his servants, 'Bring quickly the best robe, and put it on him, and put a ring on his hand, and shoes on his feet. And bring the fattened calf and kill it, and let us eat and celebrate. For this my son was dead, and is alive again; he was lost, and is found.' And they began to celebrate." (Luke 15:11–24 ESV)

Obviously, the father was the most senior dog in the story. But he doesn't have that old-dog attitude. The rigid one in this case is his oldest son.

I just need to stop here and say that, as a father, this whole story breaks my heart in so many ways. It breaks my heart that the father lost his younger boy in the first place. It breaks my heart that the prodigal son had this much love at home yet still felt he needed to leave to find something better. Sadly, I know it happens all the time; that's how freedom of choice works. But my heart really breaks for the father, and therefore breaks for God.

After teaching on this, my favorite story in the world for so many years, I started to wonder, What if the younger brother left *because* of the older brother in the first place?

> "The older brother became angry and refused to go in. So his father went out and pleaded with him. But he answered his father, 'Look! All these years I've been *slaving* for you and never disobeyed your *orders*. Yet you never gave me even a young goat so I could celebrate with my friends." (Luke 15:28–29, emphasis added)

Orders? Slaving? Is that how he sees his life? Never got to have a party? Notice that the older son doesn't address his father respectfully at all. And yet the father's reaction to this son was the same as it was with the younger: he overlooked the offense.

> "'My son,' the father said, 'you are always with me, and everything I have is yours.'" (Luke 15:31)

His response was "my son," even though his son did not address him as "father." The usual word for *son* in the Greek is *huios*, but Jesus uses *teknon* here, which is the word you'd use for a little child. It's a very tender word. This is an amazingly good father.

Dad was not the problem. Think this through with me. If you had an older brother whose attitude was that being at home was terrible and he could never have any fun, wouldn't that influence your attitude? If your older sibling thought home was just glorified slavery, you would feel like getting out of there, wouldn't you? Don't you know people like this? Maybe you work with them, or they're in your family as well. There was an old *Saturday Night Live* sketch featuring the characters Doug and Wendy Whiner, who could make any best day miserable. If they were your older siblings, you would probably want to run away too.

That's what makes me so sad for the father. From everything I can ascertain from this story, he was completely misrepresented by the older brother. I could picture him telling his older son, "Who said you couldn't have a party?! Go, get a goat. Barbecue some veal. Have your friends over. Do you even have any friends?"

If you have been a part of God's kingdom in any way and decided to leave, did you even know the true God you were leaving behind? Or could you be leaving a slave-driving, order-giving, party-less interpretation of God demonstrated to you by your older brother?

One of my friends told me that when he was a kid and people talked to him about becoming a Christian, they always said how wonderful it was going to be:

> However, once I became a Christian it seemed like things changed, and it became all about the stuff you couldn't do, instead of helping you figure out what you're supposed to live for.

165

I came up with a brief list of things that we weren't supposed to do: dancing, drinking, prom/homecoming, movies, mixed swimming, kissing, smoking, long hair, laughing or joking in church, and, of course, rock music. I remember one of the big rallying points for the churches in the area was when they pulled together to boycott Pizza Hut because they served beer—and a good Christian would never be caught dead in a restaurant that served beer.

The boycott didn't last long, however, because even uptight and legalistic Christians love pizza. So, they got their pizza to go. They snuck it out in a brown paper bag.[1]

This joyless legalism was how the older son in the story lived. Look at his words to the father: "But when this son of yours who has squandered your property with prostitutes comes home, you kill the fattened calf for him!" (Luke 15:30).

Who said anything about prostitutes? This word *prostitute* in this case could mean a woman who sells herself or just a party girl. It could simply mean "easy like Sunday morning." Here is my question: How does the older brother know that his little brother had been with wild girls? He hasn't talked to him yet. He doesn't have any idea where he's been. It's not like he's been following him on social media and saw drunk selfies on the internet.

Perhaps I'm reading too much into this because I would assume the same thing. But it makes you wonder if the older brother, in some way, was a little jealous about more than just the welcome home party. Remember also that Jesus is telling this story to the party-less church leaders who were mad that Jesus was friends with "prostitutes."

I certainly have no issue believing that part of the older

brother's problem was the waste of Dad's resources and the stupid behavior that left the younger brother in the gutter feeding pigs. Jesus was making the point that the younger brother's behavior was obviously inappropriate. I mean, he's telling this story to the Jews, and pigs are definitely un-kosher. They were on the list of unclean animals in Old Testament law after all.

However, it doesn't appear that wastefulness, disrespect, and pork contamination are really the problem for the older brother. The crux of the problem seems to be that he had to stay home and slave away, and he wishes he could have had a chance to spend at least one weekend in Vegas.

Again, I'm not condoning the behavior of the younger brother. Let me tell you again and again and again that it's much better not to make dumb decisions and end up with the pigs. It's just that even if you did end up with the pigs—or if you do end up with the pigs—the absolute best place to be is back home, as the younger son figured out. This is the incredible paradox in the story. I've talked to so many people who wish they had never left home in the first place.

But how do you convince the older brother of this fact? That you made a mistake and realized home was the best place to be? He had the same dad you did, and you both missed the gracious love of your father.

Bob George puts it this way:

> When Christians are living under law, the results are the same as they have always been. And it doesn't matter whether you are trying to live up to God's laws, man-made laws, or even your own self-imposed standards. The result will be fear, guilt, frustration, and feelings of condemnation. You

will experience a lack of ability to love God or men. How can you love a God that you are laboring to please but never can? And when you are feeling continual guilt and condemnation, how can you be kind and forgiving to other people? When they appear to be doing well, you envy them. When they fail, you judge them. After all, why should I let you off the hook if God is hammering me every time I blow it? That's the way you think under law.[2]

Many groups of Christians have chosen to live in a party-less type of relationship with God. The Amish would be the first to come to mind. They have a tradition called *Rumspringa*, which literally means a time to "run around." It is a case in point for the way they chose to live. When an Amish child hits adolescence, they are given several years to run around and not be Amish, which sounds wilder than it usually is. They are not encouraged to go crazy, as some have reported. Most of them still live at home and do things in organized youth groups. Some of the boys put stereos in their buggies (seriously, that's a thing). Just once I want to hear Wiz Khalifa blaring from an Amish buggy. But for the most part, it's just a coming-of-age experience, and it gives them the chance to decide for themselves if they want to remain in church.

I fully respect this community and their traditions of piety. It's just that I can't help but think that their relationship with their heavenly Father must feel like a grind. If they see the need to allow their children to walk away from their lifestyle for a time before they decide if they really want to sign on for it for the rest of their life, it must really be a burden to them, or at least limiting.

Whatever the case may be, my point is that if your entire existence with the heavenly Father is more about all the things you must give up, the things you don't get to do, then you had better make a *very* informed decision about your future. The Amish are an extreme example, but let's be honest, this is the same reason many young Christians walk away from faith. For them there is no official Rumspringa; they just leave. How sad that must be for Dad.

Here is another approach. What if you didn't have to leave at all? What if you can live with the ring, the robe, the BBQ, and the party while still at home with Dad? What if you didn't have to go through hell to figure out that heaven was the best place to be, and that you had it right in front of you?

Honestly, this is the best description of "religion" I've ever heard: slaving, order-obeying, and party-less. No father wants his children to live slaving or in party-lessness. Good fathers want their children to live in loving relationships. Sure, there is work to do; there are still expectations and correct ways to act and think and live. The younger brother figured out that there is no way to avoid those responsibilities. You can work for Dad or the pig farmer or yourself, but you still need to work—there is a reality to life after all.

But no father wants his kids to feel like they are "slaving" in

> If your entire existence with the heavenly Father is more about all the things you must give up, the things you don't get to do, then you had better make a *very* informed decision about your future.

169

their family existence. This is exactly the point Jesus was trying to make to the older brothers he was teaching. God has given us freedom. Freedom to travel as far away as we think we need to go to find happiness, or freedom to stay home and find happiness in the only place it really exists. If we choose the former, odds are that we're going to realize home was the better place. Jesus wants you to know the door to his home is always open. It's just too bad so many people can't figure that out unless they hit rock bottom (aka working at the pig farm).

Why does life at home with God seem like something we feel we need to run away from? Because so many of us who live with the Father make it *seem* like such a drag. These are the words of Jesus: "I have told you this [the reason I'm teaching you, like this is part of my mission] so that my joy may be in you and that your joy may be complete" (John 15:11).

In this verse and this parable, Jesus is making it clear that the problem with humanity is not that we're having too much joy and God wants us to knock it off; it's the opposite. The Father wants us to have joy, so he sent his Son to make that happen. He wants us to love our home and find it the most appealing place in the universe.

As parents, Denise and I are empty nesters. We have been for a while now. But our nest is *really* empty. We made the mistake of allowing our children to see the rest of the world as they were growing up. We felt it was pivotal that they see how people live in developing countries. Seeing the world has given them confidence and heart for helping others, and it has cultivated their passion for finding their own journeys with Jesus.

But it also led to them figuring out that there were better places to live. It turns out, Illinois is the number-one state . . .

people are moving away from. Our two daughters are in Southern California and the other one is in Nashville. It's hard to argue with their logic, but we miss them all, which makes their homecomings most sweet. When they visit, we bend over backward to have all the things they need, and all the groceries purchased (there is always good pizza; you have to maximize your strengths); I often burn my frequent flyer miles to get them back to Illinois. Even when we start to get tired and are okay with them heading back to their paradise, leaving us with some peace and quiet, we never let on, because we want them to find joy with us. We want their joy to be as complete as is humanly possible.

And that's exactly what our heavenly Father wants for us.

Blocking the Way Home

Let's go back a couple of stories to the parable of the lost sheep. In Luke 15, Jesus was telling a trilogy of stories to the older brothers: the parable of the lost sheep, the parable of the lost coin, and the parable of the lost son. These older brothers were the church leaders complaining about Jesus doing his mission, the ones he was mad at, who were actually blocking others from their way home.

> He told them this parable: "What man of you, having a hundred sheep, if he has lost one of them, does not leave the ninety-nine in the open country, and go after the one that is lost, until he finds it? And when he has found it, he lays it on his shoulders, rejoicing. And when he comes home, he calls together his friends and his neighbors, saying to them,

'Rejoice with me, for I have found my sheep that was lost.'
Just so, I tell you, there will be more joy in heaven over one
sinner who repents than over ninety-nine righteous persons
who need no repentance." (Luke 15:3–7 ESV)

There is a very telling piece of information in the middle of
this sheep story that goes along with the older brother's attitude.
Did you catch it? It's the phrase "open country."

Jesus didn't say the shepherd left the ninety-nine sheep in
the safety of a sheep pen, or mention the sheep being in the
company of another shepherd. They are left in the open country.
They are left in danger. If the shepherd gets lost or hurt, they
may have to fend for themselves. Not a strong point for sheep.

As you know, sheep are defenseless creatures. Rabbits run,
dogs bite, horses kick, cats scratch, and skunks . . . do their thing.
But sheep can't bite, kick, scratch, or burrow into the ground to
hide. They have no defense mechanism. They don't have claws,
and they can't spray you with deadly poison. They are lunch for
predators. This is the reason why sheep need a shepherd. Many
other animals can be left by themselves for a long period of time,
but sheep need constant care and protection.

Ironically, as badly as sheep need a shepherd, they hardly
ever cooperate with him. They are very rebellious, untrainable,
ignorant animals. You would think they would appreciate the
one protecting them, but no. Dumb and Dumber. This is why
you never see dancing sheep at a circus. I got to see Russian
dancing bears in a circus one time. They were so human-like it
was hard to tell whether they were really bears or small people in
bear suits. Bears can protect themselves quite well, *and* they are
trainable. Da Bears!

But sheep are defenseless _and_ uncooperative, which is why being a shepherd was one of the lowest of all occupations. Nobody wants the job. I tried it one fateful day at a little Dutch theme park in Holland, Michigan. They had candle dipping, a petting zoo, and cheese making (blessed are the cheese makers). On this day, one of the sheep carefully executed a clever escape and was wandering free through the outlet mall next door. He evidently swam through a little pond and broke out. He must have been desperate, because sheep hate water, according to the worker I decided to help.

A couple of ladies in long dresses and wooden shoes and I figured that the only way to get this animal back in the fold was to get him to jump back into the water. Now, suffice it to say that the little lamb chop had been in the water once and had no intention of going back. So, everywhere we went, the lamb was sure _not_ to go (Mary was nowhere to be found). Just as we got him cornered, he would cut through us and escape again. He was too fast to catch and too dumb to realize that life would be better for him in the barn than it ever could be at the Nike outlet.

And then it hit me. Sheep are stupid. When Jesus said, "I am the shepherd and you are the sheep," it wasn't a compliment! Sheep don't know what's best for them. That is why the shepherd needs to lead them to the still water and green pastures. Otherwise, they'll go shopping.

Thus, the reason why the Bible personifies them as people. Isaiah 53:6 says, "We all, like sheep, have gone astray, each of us has turned to our own way." And Matthew 9:36 says that Jesus looked out into the crowd and had compassion on them, because he saw them as "sheep without a shepherd."

So Jesus told these three stories in Luke 15 with the point being: "'Rejoice with me; I have found my lost sheep.' I tell you that in the same way there will be more rejoicing in heaven over one sinner who repents than over ninety-nine righteous persons who do not need to repent" (Luke 15:6–7).

Jesus came for the lost sheep, which never makes the other ninety-nine happy. And it probably never will.

Epilogue on the Older Brother

What ended up happening to the older brother? How did things turn out for the sheep? Let's return to the story. Remember where we left him? He was angry that his father was celebrating his brother's return, when he never did anything like that for him while he was slaving at home. Resentment just oozed from this son. What he really meant was, "What about me?"

- "You killed the fatted calf for him . . . but what about me?"
- "You threw a party for him . . . but what about for me?"
- "You gave him the best robe . . . but what about one for me?"

The other lost lamb was broken, not proud. He came home with his head down, bruised, bleeding, beaten. He'd been at the outlet mall long enough. What he needed was a place of love, acceptance, and healing. When he came back home, he found that with the father, but not with his brother.

Let me just say that I have heard from the older brothers many times in thirty-five years of working at the church:

- "But I like the old way we did it."
- "Why do we want more people here? I like things the way they are!"
- "We should be taking more care of those who are already in the church." (I was once accused by one of my leaders of bringing too many new people into this church.)

The older-brother mentality is the spirit of resentment that says, "What about me?!"

There is a difference between the story of the lost son and the lost sheep in that the Father didn't go searching for his son. I think it's because it wouldn't have done any good. In this case, the son had to come home of his own free will.

But God's priority in both stories is obvious: finding the one who is lost.

CHAPTER 14

WHEN CHRISTIANS GET IN THE WAY

You've Been Galileo'd

"You study the Scriptures diligently because you think that in them you have eternal life. These are the very Scriptures that testify about me, yet you refuse to come to me to have life."

(JOHN 5:39–40)

Then Jesus said to the crowds and to his disciples: "The teachers of the law and the Pharisees sit in Moses' seat. So you must be careful to do everything they tell you. But do not do what they do, for they do not practice what they preach. They tie up heavy, cumbersome loads and put them on other people's shoulders, but they themselves are not willing to lift a finger to move them."

(MATT. 23:1–4)

One of the experts in the law answered him, "Teacher, when you say these things, you insult us also."

Jesus replied, "And you experts in the law, woe to

you, because you load people down with burdens they can
hardly carry, and you yourselves will not lift one finger
to help them."

(LUKE 11:45–46)

HAVE YOU EVER SEEN A church with a No Trespassing sign in front of it? I have. I know it's something their insurance carrier must have forced them to put up, but when I saw it I thought to myself, *That's the problem exactly!* There used to be a sign on the fence of a convent in California that said, "No trespassing—violators will be prosecuted to the full extent of the law," and it was signed "Sisters of Mercy."

When I came to the church where I currently serve in Chicagoland in 1990, it might as well have had a No Trespassing sign in front of it. As a matter of fact, there was this wonderful old deacon who had been suggesting for years that we needed a fence and a gate around our property. He was the one that usually cleaned up the messes left by the neighborhood kids, so I know he was just being practical. But when one of our church leaders refused to let some of the kids come in and use the bathroom one day, we had to have a discussion about things.

Denied access is what made Jesus angry, because our mission is to help people get in, not to keep them out. Access is the key. God wants his kingdom to be easy to get into. He paid a high price for this barrier-free access, so let's get it right.

I feel the same way about access even in practical ways. For example, my garage door was once bent and banged up for reasons I'm not allowed to share publicly. So the laser safety sensors had a hard time making a connection around the bent door. I never liked those sensors. I hate it when, after hitting the close button, I have to run fast to the door while doing that little dance over the beam so it won't go back up. I'm not a good dancer.

I know they are safety devices, but I want easy access to my house. At one point I'd had enough and decided to try to disconnect them, which didn't work. Some branch of OSHA forced the manufacturer to make the device tamper-proof. They were made to thwart unsafe people like me, I guess. At this point, I literally couldn't use the door, so I tried to work around it by splicing the wires together, but OSHA was ahead of me there too. Then, in a really bad moment, I just duct-taped the sensors to the wall right next to each other so they wouldn't sense anything. It worked, but I quickly felt convicted that perhaps safety was important, so I got a new door.

As terribly dumb and dangerous as this illustration may be, I'd like for you to think of those sensors symbolically with me for a minute. We were separated from God when Adam and Eve sinned. Ever since then, God has been on one side of the garage door and mankind on the other. Jesus' sacrifice gave us the garage door opener to get in. But the evil one is constantly banging his car into the door to keep the device from working, trying to make it harder to get in. Sometimes he is overt, and sometimes he is subversive. His best tactic, unfortunately, is to use God's other children to mess up the door, denying access to the Father. Jesus said of them, "They are blind guides leading the blind" (Matt. 15:14 NLT).

Don't think I haven't pondered this a great deal as I wrote this book. What if I'm also blind? I can tell you that I have thought about, prayed for, and studied this issue my entire life. I believe that when Jesus taught us to pray to our Father in heaven, it was groundbreaking theology. No religious system saw God that way. And when he said that God is a fantastic Father—the Father who gives good gifts (Matt. 7:11)—he really meant it; God is a God of gifts. If all that is true, then my job as a church leader is to make it as simple as possible to get the door open.

John 3:16–17 puts it this way:

> For God so loved the world that he gave his one and only Son, that whoever believes in him shall not perish but have eternal life. For God did not send his Son into the world to condemn the world, but to save the world through him.

And Luke 14:23 says this:

> "Then the master told his servant, 'Go out to the roads and country lanes and compel them to come in, so that my house will be full.'"

My job is to fix the door so everyone can immediately get in. My job is to help people come back to the welcome home party our Father has waiting for them (Luke 15:22–24). My job is to create a barrier-free access to God.

My job is *not* to follow in the footsteps of the Pharisees, with whom Jesus was so often frustrated:

> "Woe to you, teachers of the law and Pharisees, you hypocrites! You shut the door of the kingdom of heaven in people's faces. You yourselves do not enter, nor will you let those enter who are trying to." (Matt. 23:13–14)

The Pharisees *thought* they were entering the kingdom by following the rules, when in fact they were bending the garage door and making it harder to get in. They just never got it. They ended up shutting the door in people's faces because, unfortunately, there was no other way to get in—Jesus was, and is, the only way.

How did they not know this? I need to know how they could have missed it so I don't make the same mistake. The answer is that these church leaders stood in the doorway with a religious *system*. Instead of helping people understand how much God loved them, they created a greater barrier.

As transparent as I'm trying to be in this book, let me admit one of my own worst episodes of door slamming. It had to do with science. Science has come a long way since Jesus' time, which is a wonderful advantage to the world in so many ways. However, it has also created new ways to block access to God, to bang up the garage door.

When Jesus said, "Woe to you, teachers," there were way fewer ways for those teachers to slam the door than we have today. Intellectual door slamming wasn't nearly as big a problem back then, because church leaders were usually the most educated people around. They were at least on par with any Roman or Greek intellectuals. At that point in history, it was just as difficult for Greek scholars to prove that Atlas was holding the world on his shoulders as it was for Jewish scholars to prove that Jehovah God placed it in the sky.

Today it's much different. Most of the folks I encounter who have doubts about God have some degree of scientific, intellectual issues with the Bible and, therefore, of their understanding of God. They have been taught that science and the Bible can't coexist, which is a big problem. Mortimer Adler, one of the greatest thinkers of the twentieth century, said that the question of the existence of God is the most important question a person could ask, because more consequences follow from the way you answer that question than any other question in life.[1]

To be clear, there are plenty of scientists who believe in God, and some feel they can reconcile science and the Bible without problem. The number of scientists who believe in God has stayed consistent throughout recent history:

> In 1916, researchers asked biologists, physicists, and mathematicians whether they believed in a God who actively communicates with humankind and to whom one may pray in expectation of receiving an answer. About 40 percent answered in the affirmative. In 1997, the same survey was repeated verbatim—and to the surprise of the researchers, the percentage remained very nearly the same.[2]

What I'm saying is that science doesn't have to be a problem. A large percentage of scientific doubt has not been caused by new scientific knowledge; it's been caused by how Christians, like me, have interpreted the Bible in light of scientific knowledge.

Many of us have shut the door on many people who believe in science. I was part of the problem for a while. My trouble was that I had never learned about any scientific evidence that pointed to God, so when I did, I wanted others to know about it. I grew up hearing that evolution was a crazy idea and couldn't be proven. So I accepted it and rolled my eyes when it was brought up. But along the way, I was given the chance to study what science does and doesn't say about God, and I found that there were some reputable scientists who reconciled science and the Bible in some interesting ways. It bolstered my faith as I read their scientific evidence for God. This was new information for me at the time.

I preached a sermon series on it, invited guest lecturers, wrote a paper on creationism for a graduate class, and honestly acted like I knew more than I really did (which is also what I'm doing writing this book, but that's beside the point). It's human nature to want to be right, and the only reason there is a comment section on any form of social media.

Then one day I had a life-changing lunch with a good friend of mine. If you had me make a short list of people I'd want to be stranded on a desert island with, this guy would definitely be on my list. He's fun, funny, interesting, in a heavy metal band, and has a PhD. If he had been on Gilligan's Island, they would have been rescued immediately. I'm not saying building a radio from a coconut wasn't cool, but this guy would have put the professor to shame.

My friend was exploring Christianity at the time he heard me spouting off about my new scientific knowledge. He asked me a question that changed my paradigm; it literally changed my ministry. He asked, "Do I have to believe in your version of creation to be a Christian?" This was really a deeper question than just this one issue. He was asking, What *does* one need to believe to be a Christian? Do I have to recant my scientific understanding to be a Christian?

"Well," I said, pausing, "I guess . . . not."

What I knew was that in my study, I'd read various theories by Christian scientists from all kinds of backgrounds. Some tried to refute Darwinian evolution with science, some explained evolution with a biblical perspective, and some were complete theistic evolutionists, meaning they believed God *was* the big bang. I found the latter category a little confusing, considering

A large percentage of scientific doubt has not been caused by new scientific knowledge; it's been caused by how Christians, like me, have interpreted the Bible in light of scientific knowledge.

my understanding of Scripture and the claim that God created everything according to its own kind (Gen. 1:24–25). I had to admit, though, that some of them seemed to have a much deeper understanding of God in their own ways—and that they were *all* smarter than me.

When my friend asked me the question, it forced me to realize that it just didn't matter. It was as if the voice of God was asking me, "Do you really think I would want one of my children to find a closed garage door because of *your* interpretation of something that happened a long time ago? Something that no one will ever be able to answer?"

"No, sir."

Is there going to be a hobbled old man at the pearly gates demanding, "Answer me, these questions three."[3] Probably not. But if there is, I seriously doubt this would be one of the questions.

> Now faith is confidence in what we hope for and assurance about what we do not see. . . .
>
> By faith we understand that the universe was formed at God's command, so that what is seen was not made out of what was visible. (Heb. 11:1, 3)

That was yet another time when I might have fallen into the category of what made Jesus angry. I might have heard him say, "You shut the door of the kingdom of heaven in people's faces."

Do You Know Galileo?

Have you ever heard of Galileo, the Italian astronomer and physicist? In 1633, the church condemned him for spreading heresy and forced him to recant. The story involved more than a little politics as well, but basically the church said, "Oh, we know you are really smart, Galileo, and hundreds of years from now people will still know your name and acknowledge the amazing breakthroughs you made in science. But we are the church, and we know everything."

The issue? The church believed the Bible clearly taught that the earth was the center of the universe and that the sun revolved around it. This had been the accepted teaching of science and the church up to this point. By the way, in case you flunked out of science, that's not true.

Ultimately the data and the consistency of the theory's predictions convinced even the most skeptical scientists. The Catholic Church remained strongly opposed, however, claiming that this view was incompatible with Holy Scripture. In retrospect, it is clear that the scriptural basis for those claims was remarkably thin; nonetheless, this confrontation raged for decades and ultimately did considerable harm, both to science and to the church.[4]

The above quote is from Francis Collins, a scientist who believes in God. He was one of the scientists given the task of mapping DNA. In his book about the process of deciphering DNA, *The Language of God*, he presents some of the best arguments I've ever read on behalf of a creator God.

In an event celebrating this milestone with the world, then president Clinton called DNA the "language of God," which was obviously controversial within scientific communities. But Collins agreed, and basically said the same thing in his speech:

> What was going on here? Why would a president and a scientist, charged with announcing a milestone in biology and medicine, feel compelled to invoke a connection with God? Aren't the scientific and spiritual worldviews antithetical, or shouldn't they at least avoid appearing in the East Room together? What were the reasons for invoking God in these two speeches? Was this poetry? Hypocrisy? A cynical attempt to curry favor from believers, or to disarm those who might criticize this study of the human genome as reducing humankind to machinery? No. Not for me. Quite the contrary, for me the experience of sequencing the human genome, and uncovering this most remarkable of all texts, was both a stunning scientific achievement and an occasion of worship.[5]

The above is an excerpt from the beginning of his book. In the following several hundred pages, Collins proceeds to present his reasons for believing in theistic evolution, that God started the process. I still don't agree, or even understand, why God would use a long, slow evolutionary process. But the bigger question is this: Could this really smart scientist be a Christian if he does believe that?

As I was pondering about my friend, Francis Collins, and Galileo, it dawned on me that even though we know a lot more now about how the solar system works, many kingdom doors are still being slammed shut because the church thinks everything revolves around them. Why did the church believe the sun revolved around the earth 400 years ago, you may ask? Because the Bible plainly says so: "God, the LORD, speaks and summons the earth from the rising of the sun to the place where it sets" (Ps. 50:1).

So the church told Galileo, "Mr. Galileo, the Bible says the sun rises and sets. That settles it. I believe it, and you must believe it also. Your *new* science cannot be true." As we know, church leaders can be narrow-minded.

Let's not forget that Copernicus started this revolution (that placed the sun rather than the earth at the center of the universe), which Galileo championed. Later, Isaac Newton added math to the equation. By then it started to become obvious to everyone that the church had been wrong all those years, which forced the church to either admit they were wrong (something that is always hard for narrow-minded people to do) or just hang on to their incorrect interpretation of Scripture. Guess what they did? They created a barrier for rational people who now had an intellectual doubt in God for absolutely no reason. Was the Bible wrong, or had they missed something in their interpretation?

The reason I love this story is that, 400 years later, we still use the terms *sunrise* and *sunset*. Check your weather app or ask Siri what time the sun will set today. Does Siri really believe that the sun sets? Or is it just an expression? As a church leader, and as a rational human being, the simple response is that the psalmist wasn't trying to argue science, and the Bible wasn't written to define astronomy or explain the origin of the earth. So why did I think *I* needed to do that?

Let me say that there are plenty of people who have legitimate doubts about God after they have studied the Bible and science. My point is that many people have been shut out of the kingdom—they have been Galileo'd into intellectual doubts—by narrow-minded Christians with narrow-minded views. This must be incredibly frustrating to our Father, who just wants us all to come home.

We can't possibly think that God cares whether we believe he created the world with a bang, or in six literal days, or in 600 million years. What he cares about is that we come home. And that we know that the door is open. He didn't send his Son all the way to our little planet so we could come home, only to find me and my interpretations blocking the way!

Paul wrote, "Don't have anything to do with foolish and stupid arguments, because you know they produce quarrels. And the Lord's servant must not be quarrelsome but must be kind to everyone, able to teach, not resentful" (2 Tim. 2:23–24).

And Peter said, "But in your hearts revere Christ as Lord. Always be prepared to give an answer to everyone who asks you to give the reason for the hope that you have. But do this with gentleness and respect" (1 Peter 3:15).

Let me point out that it is also very important to understand the culture we live in as we live out our faith. When Peter got up to preach his very first sermon in Acts 2, he used a lot of insider language because he was preaching to an all-Jewish audience.

The crucifixion of Jesus had just happened; everyone listening to him knew that happened. So he went at them pretty hard.

The apostle Paul preached differently, depending on his audience. When he got to Athens in Acts 17, he addressed an intellectual crowd full of people from diverse backgrounds by starting with one small connection point, a statue to an "unknown God" (Acts 17:23). He took a noncombative stance and used logic instead of rhetoric. He didn't try to argue with them. He had to open the door.

My point is that, Toto, we don't live in Acts 2 anymore. Perhaps we should keep the nonessential things out of the way.

I've already told you about my wonderful British son-in-law, Ash. What I didn't tell you is that it took more than beer with some Christians to get him to come around. He had a lot of these intellectual barriers as well. My daughter Rachel is great at breaking down barriers; she's a natural at starting with an "unknown God statue" to find connection. Let me insert you into one of the dialogues she and Ash had from separate continents as their friendship developed.

One day Ash got pretty vulnerable and said,

I've spent twenty-two years wishing people would take my word as truth, and it really got to a point where almost everyone did. If people questioned me, I'd just bury them so they wouldn't try it again. But do you know what I realized? I throw feelings into explanations. I do have feelings. I just don't know how to deal with them. So I find a justification in my head. Then I throw the feelings into the justification bag and put it in the cupboard. Then I don't have to address it.

(I didn't realize I also did that until just a few years ago. I told you he was smart.)

> Usually those justifications aren't valid, and I never challenge them. But if other people challenge them, I fight hard and usually I win. But you don't challenge me, Rachel. You don't tell me I'm wrong, you just . . . I don't know. It's like you sit and wait for me to realize how stupid I am, and then I do! And I challenge my own justifications.
>
> I mean, look at Christianity. When I met you, I could have, and had in the past, given you hours of justification for why I hated religion. I could have reeled off a list and put some religious fanatics in their places. And had you come at me and challenged why I hated religion, challenged why I pitied people who believed in God and Jesus and the resurrection, I would have put you in your place and, no offense, I would probably have come away looking pretty smug for all my excellent arguments and rational victories of logic. But you didn't do that. You just went ahead and showed me that it was all bull$#@%. And that most of my facts are opinions wrapped in justification.
>
> Well the best analogy I can think of is kind of biblical, but I'm going to risk it. It's like I spent years building all these foundations to stand on, and people would come and say, "Hey, your foundations are looking pretty rubbish." And I'd throw stuff at them and tell them to bugger off. They were, after all, just standing in the mud. Then you walk up and, instead of making fun of my rubbish foundations, you just walk over and stand on a rock. I'm looking over, thinking, *Hang on. She's not saying it, but . . . that rock required no*

building at all. And it looks sturdier than my foundations. And you haven't got to tell me, because I can see the dumb rock.

There are so many issues to argue about, and so little fruit to gain from arguing. I mean, Rachel and Ash had some great spiritual conversations (still do). I'm not insinuating that we don't talk about spiritual things at all. I think it's just much better to start by standing on the Rock. Show them what Jesus looks like—let your light shine.

CONCLUSION

When Guilt Gets in the Way

Creating Free Access to the Father's Love

AS I'VE SAID THROUGHOUT THIS book, although I know many of us picture Jesus as some kind of hippie from the sixties, he legitimately got angry at people. But never at the people who had questions about God, or the obvious sinners. He was always mad at the religious people.

We may dismiss that now, because we see those people as the ones who didn't really get who God was—and actually killed Jesus. But so much of what he talked about still applies to religion today. And we can better understand his passion when we see that people's issues with God actually come down to religion, and their understanding of him comes out of an incorrect representation. Think about it this way:

- Most of our intellectual issues are probably based on an incorrect human interpretation of God.
- Most of our emotional issues are probably based on an incorrect human interpretation of God.
- Most of our religious issues are probably based on an incorrect human interpretation of God.

However, when I'm asked questions about God, what I find is that, most of the time, the questions aren't really about God at all. They are about religion. And religion, as we have made it to be, has caused incredible damage. Here is the problem: the longer we play the game of religion, the better we think we are at it; and the harder it is to let go.

Back in the day, when text, phone, and cell minutes were much more closely regulated, I decided to check on my cell phone plan. Imagine my surprise when I found out I had 6,000 rollover minutes, time I had paid for but hadn't used. I was obviously paying for a plan that gave me more access to the phone than my family needed. I was wasting money.

So I called my phone company and said to the salesperson, "Okay, how can I save some money here? I should probably downgrade my plan, right?"

She told me that I could, but then I would lose my 6,000 rollover minutes.

I told her to do it anyway.

Then the nice woman on the phone said, "I'm really glad to hear you say that, because a lot of people wouldn't do it."

I asked, "Why? Why wouldn't people switch and save money?"

She said, "Some people just can't give up their rollover minutes."

That's how the church leaders looked at religion: "But, Jesus, we have 6,000 rollover minutes! We have tithed this and prayed that and gone without stuff and gotten up early and stayed up late to get these points. But if we follow you, we lose them."

So, even though the new plan is a lot better, they just couldn't let the old one go. Obviously, the people who didn't have enough minutes flocked to Jesus. But the ones who thought they were doing well had a hard time switching, even though it was a much, much better plan.

Ironically, this problem keeps happening. Even for people who follow Jesus. They get stuck in their version of the plan. Even though we know God says we don't need that plan. Jesus died to save us from the plan. He canceled the plan. To use Paul's language: "Having canceled the charge of our legal indebtedness, which stood against us and condemned us; he has taken it away, nailing it to the cross" (Col. 2:14).

It's just so hard to let go of our religion, which leads to pride, which leads to judgment, which leads to barriers to God. People who know they need God but don't feel good about their relationship with him, need us to help them understand how great the new plan is so we would all switch over.

For some reason, many people are surprised when they find out I'm a pastor. I get it. I don't present like a "man of the cloth." Once they find out, I can instantly read their reaction, whether positive or negative. I can't tell you how many times I've heard the "get the [blank] out of here" response to the revelation. That's my favorite. Occasionally, I see some form of shock as the blood drains from their faces. Meeting a member of the clergy creates instantaneous guilt, like I'm an undercover agent for the HBI (the Heavenly Bureau of Investigation). Busted.

One night I was driving late on a strange road when police lights started flashing behind me. I had been speeding; it's one of my spiritual gifts. As it turns out, my car tag had also expired. Oh yeah, and I had failed to change the address on my driver's license to my new residence of about a year, which was why I didn't get the car tag notice in the first place. Three strikes. This couldn't be good.

The officer looked at my commercial driver's license and proceeded to give me a lecture on why a "professional" driver should be more careful. I probably should have just said, "Yes, sir," but I'm also smart enough to play the "get out of jail free" card if I can do it. So I proceeded to explain to him that I wasn't really a commercial driver, to which I knew the follow-up question would be, "Then why do you have a CDL?" Indeed, he fell into my plan.

"Well, I'm a pastor, and I have to have the commercial license to drive our church bus." Play 'em if you got 'em.

I'm guessing not many of you have had the opportunity to observe a police officer feel guilty for pulling *you* over. He was speechless. He looked like he'd just pulled over the mayor, who was going to call his superior and get him in trouble.

Finally, he said, "Oh . . . you're a pastor. Well, just a minute," and went back to his car. After a few minutes, he came up to the window again and said, "I just can't give you a ticket. You should be more careful, but I just can't give you a ticket."

Not wanting to argue, I just said, "Oh, okay, I'm sorry. I'll get all this fixed."

He followed with, "I haven't been to confession in years." He then went on to lament about how disappointing it must be to his Italian mother that he didn't go to church anymore. (I promise this is a true story.)

I realized then that, in some way, my irresponsible driving habits were in actuality a gift from God as an answer to a mother's prayer. We had a nice conversation about God and religion, and I invited him to church and gave him my card. I have since installed a little curtain on the driver-side door I can pull closed for confession in case it ever happens again.

I must admit I drove away feeling very conflicted. I was definitely relieved about my acquittal, but I was also disappointed for the officer and his relationship with his heavenly Father. He seemed like someone who had let his phone bill go unpaid for so long that he thought it was shut off. Maybe he couldn't possibly compete with his mom, so he gave up. I think deep inside he—we all—really wants to be close to God. It's just so difficult when we think it's conditional upon our behavior.

C. S. Lewis, in his book *Mere Christianity*, wrote of a schoolboy who was asked what he thought God was like: "The boy replied that as far as he could make out, God was the sort of person who was always snooping around to see if anyone was enjoying themselves and trying to stop it."[1]

My premise here is that God loves you, and what made Jesus mad was when someone denied your access to that love. Maybe you didn't get the experience of living with a good father, like I did. But even if you had the best father in the world, he doesn't hold a candle to your heavenly Father. I'm sorry if the thought of God makes you feel guilty. Jesus knows him better than any of us, and he said that earthly fathers have limited ability for good, but "how much more will your Father in heaven give good gifts to those who ask him!" (Matt. 7:11). How much more!

Usually, if you grow up with some sort of faith background, God has Santa Claus–type status in the beginning. He is great and good and does nice things for you, but you never get to see him or know him or even meet him. (Going to the mall to meet Santa who smells like beef and cheese doesn't really help.) Unfortunately, many people never grow out of this image of God, so at whatever point he fails to bring them their Christmas pony, they start to have belief problems.

When you're a teen or young adult, your idea of God can go one of two ways. He is either becoming the real heavenly Father you have longed for, or things get worse and he becomes Angry Santa, the personification of rules and regulations you do not understand and have zero desire to follow. Angry Santa is "making a list and checking it twice," and you realize how naughty you have been. All of a sudden, bada-boom bada-bing, you have yourself a terrible image of God.

[Jesus] said that earthly fathers have limited ability for good, but "how much more will your Father in heaven give good gifts to those who ask him!" (Matt. 7:11)

My favorite old *Saturday Night Live* sketch was "Deep Thoughts with Jack Handy." It was just random sentences scrolling on the screen as ethereal music played in the background. One of my favorite lines was, "If a kid asks where rain comes from, I think a cute thing to tell him is 'God is crying.' And if he asks why God is crying, another cute thing to tell him is, 'Probably because of something you did.'"

That's the problem. I tried to explain this error to my new cop friend. I hope he has it figured out by now. Jesus came to obliterate the idea of a snooping-around God who is bent on keeping you from enjoying yourself.

> Whoever does not love does not know God, because God is love. This is how God showed his love among us: He sent his one and only Son into the world that we might live through him. (1 John 4:8–9)

As Socrates taught, it is almost impossible to educate someone with an answer until he or she is invested in asking a question. So many people today don't even want to ask the question about God because they have been given the wrong answer their entire lives. That's what made Jesus angry. And I'm certain that it still does.

Dallas Willard wrote in his book *The Divine Conspiracy*,

> The acid test for any theology is this: Is the God presented one that can be loved, heart, soul, mind, and strength? If the thoughtful, honest answer is, "Not really," then we need to look elsewhere or deeper. It does not really matter how sophisticated intellectually or doctrinally our approach is. If it fails to set a lovable God—a radiant, happy, friendly, accessible, and totally competent being—before ordinary people, we have gone wrong. We should not keep going in the same direction, but turn around and take another road.[2]

Let's not be afraid to do just that. If we find ourselves walking down the same road as the ones who made Jesus mad all those years ago, let's have the courage and humility to stop, turn around, and get back onto the road toward the loving Father whose heart has always been to seek and to save.

ACKNOWLEDGMENTS

THIS BOOK HAS BEEN IN the works for over ten years. I'm not one of those people who say God laid something on my heart easily. I think he does it a lot more than I realize, but I don't often play that card on other people. I am, however, certain that God laid this book on my heart and in my brain. It's another one of those writer stories where I tried and tried to get it published back in the day but couldn't find a publisher to take it, so I sat on it. I actually published a different book along the way. I'm deeply grateful to Rick Warren and Saddleback for publishing *Life on Mission* for me in 2014, both because of the way the project helped so many churches and the increased platform it gave me to get this one published. One random night in Rwanda changed my whole world, Pastor Rick. Thank you for that.

I need to thank two friends who helped me start this project. (Some of the phrases in this book may be theirs.) Dave Latko and Earl Merkel, thank you for your work and encouragement.

This project is the product of a fantastic team of editors and brains at Thomas Nelson. Jessica Wong walked this book all the way through with me and encouraged me, all the while trying to piece together my randomness. Sujin Hong helped by getting down to the nitty gritty, and Aryn VanDyke is the marketing mastermind. Randy Frazee, thank you for the encouragement to write and for connecting me with this team.

I'm so grateful to my agent Steve Green for taking me as a client when he was in the busiest time of his life. I'm grateful for the encouragement from all the people who wrote endorsements for this book, and the many who couldn't make it happen for different reasons. I haven't had many detractors yet, let the games begin. . . .

I have three amigos who have partnered with me to do life and ministry and hold me accountable for the past fourteen years. We call ourselves the Stinklings because J. R. R. Tolkien and C. S. Lewis had a group they called the Inklings—we aren't worthy, but we liked the idea. Greg Nettle, Ben Cachiaras, and Eddie Lowen, you are my band of brothers.

My larger band of brothers is amazing. Pastor friends who continually speak into my life. If I started naming each of you, I'm sure I'd leave someone out, so I'll leave it at that. But you know who you are. I value what we do together.

My elders at Parkview are also my support network in so many ways. In a day when so many pastors either skip this important part of church leadership or have adversarial relationships with them, I just have good friends.

The staff at Parkview is unbelievable. I know that someday I'll have to retire and leave them alone, but I don't know what I'll do without them. My assistant Cris has worked tirelessly to help get this project done. She manages me, and she should get an honorary MBA for it. Bill Brown basically keeps all of it together as our executive pastor. Bill, your friendship and perfectly gifted mix of style and fun and leadership make everything work. I can't thank you enough. Wayne, Laurie, and Dan—you complete us. Casey, Chaz, Adam, Sean, and all of you who spoke into this project, I am grateful.

Mark Jones, thank you for sending sermons out every week to a bunch of random pastors. You really sparked some parts of this book at very important times.

Kyle Idleman needs to write his own books, not just write the forewords for everyone else. Thank you for taking the time to do this for me, Kyle. I owe you big time. Ken and Kaylene, thanks for raising him and partially raising me at Ozark Christian College.

Thank you, family, for your encouragement. Mom and dad, your example in this issue and love for me is immeasurable. I have watched you navigate so much of this stuff through your ministry and have seen you go through so many changes. You are examples of people who aren't always comfortable with the changes that need to happen but love them, because people find Jesus as they change. Don and Carol, I couldn't ask for more encouragement from my in-laws. I love you. Doug and Jack, brothers-in-law and brothers in the ministry, I don't know where I'd be without you both. Patti and Michele, thank you for letting them hang with me even though you knew I probably wasn't going to be all that great of an influence. Jay and Dana, it's been a joy to have you in my life. Coming from a very different perspective on Christianity, you have forced me to rethink a lot of things. Jay, thank you for being in our life.

Rachel, Lauren, and Becca, thank you for giving me the amazing privilege of being your father. You have taught me more about God than anything else in my life. I could not be prouder of you and what God has birthed in each of your lives. Rachel, thank you for your help in writing this book. You are gifted beyond what you know. Ash, Tommy, and Andy—the married sons of Harlow—thank you for completing the ensemble so well. I didn't really think I wanted sons until I met you. Thank you for loving my girls and raising my grandchildren.

Denise . . . only the good Lord knows what it's been like to be married to me for thirty-five years. I can hardly write everything I feel in love and gratitude for all your support, and your encouragement and partnership in the ministry, which has always been a team effort for us—as is this book. I can't imagine what my life would be without you. Inconceivable!

To my readers, if you are still reading this part, well, you are kind of a stalker—but thank you for picking this thing up. (I hope it's not off a shelf at Goodwill.) I know you could be doing something else with your time. Thank you for sharing it with me.

NOTES

Introduction: Getting in the Way of God's Love

1. Ridley Scott, dir., *Gladiator*, Universal Pictures, 2000.
2. Used with permission.
3. Charles Dickens, *A Christmas Carol* (New York: Bantam Classics, 1986), 62–63.
4. Barna Group, "Christians: More Like Jesus or Pharisees?" June 3, 2013, https://www.barna.com/research /christians-more-like-jesus-or-pharisees/.

Chapter 2: When Being Good Gets in the Way

1. The Yadayim is a section from a book of Jewish teaching called the Mishnah, sixth division. The section is all about handwashing (yadayim is the Hebrew word for "hands."). Jacob Neusner, *The Mishnah: A New Translation* (New Haven, CT: Yale University Press, 1988), 1123–31.
2. *The Office*, Season 2, Episode 12, "The Injury," air date January 12, 2006, written by Mindy Kaling.

Chapter 3: When Rules Get in the Way

1. *The Simpsons*, Season 7, Episode 24, "Homerpalooza," air date May 19, 1996, written by Brent Forrester.
2. Grant R. Jeffrey, *The Signature of God* (Toronto: Frontier Research Publications, 1996), 156.
3. My paraphrase from Andy Stanley's "Jesus Says" sermon in the Follow series, http://followseries.org/jesus-says.

4. Stanley, "Jesus Says" sermon.

5. Henry Clay Whitney and Abraham Lincoln, *Life and Works of Abraham Lincoln: Speeches and Presidential Addresses 1859–1865* (New York: The Current Literature Publishing Co, 1907), 273.

6. Used with permission.

7. Steve Brown, *A Scandalous Freedom: The Radical Nature of the Gospel* (West Monroe, LA: Howard, 2004), 82.

Chapter 4: When Morals Get in the Way

1. Timothy Keller, *Generous Justice: How God's Grace Makes Us Just* (New York: Penguin, 2012), 82.

2. The word *disfigure* (*aphanizō*) is literally "make invisible," a vivid expression for making unrecognizable, either by covering the head or by smearing with ash and dirt. R. T. France, *Matthew: An Introduction and Commentary* (Downers Grove, IL: InterVarsity, 1985), 1:142.

Chapter 5: When Hypocrisy Gets in the Way

1. Bob Goff, *Everybody Always: Becoming Love in a World Full of Setbacks and Difficult People* (Nashville: Nelson Books, 2018), 60.

2. Portia Nelson, *There's a Hole in My Sidewalk: The Romance of Self-Discovery* (Hillsboro, OR: Beyond Words, 1993), xi–xii.

Chapter 6: When Tradition Gets in the Way

1. Used with permission.

2. Sandee LaMotte, "No Amount of Alcohol Is Good for Your Overall Health, Global Study Says," CNN.com, https://www.cnn.com/2018/08/23/health/global-alcohol-study/index.html (accessed January 3, 2019).

3. Used with permission.

Chapter 8: When Graceless Religion Gets in the Way

1. William Barclay, *Gospel of John* (Edinburgh: Saint Andrew Press, 2001), 2:451.

2. Bob George, *Classic Christianity: Life's Too Short to Miss the Real Thing* (Eugene, OR: Harvest House, 1989), 125.

Chapter 9: When Prejudice Gets in the Way

1. Steven Sample, *The Contrarian's Guide to Leadership* (San Francisco: Jossey-Bass, 2002), 28.

2. According to rabbinic literature, to convert to Judaism, a Samaritan must first and foremost renounce any belief in the sanctity of Mount Gerizim. From *Tractate Kutim*, cited in Sacha Stern, *Jewish Identity in Early Rabbinic Writings* (Leiden: Brill, 1997), 105.

Chapter 10: When Neighbors and Gnats Get in the Way

1. Elias Chacour, *Blood Brothers* (Grand Rapids: Baker, 2013), 98.

2. Donald Miller, *Blue Like Jazz: Nonreligious Thoughts on Christian Spirituality* (Nashville: Thomas Nelson, 2003), 22.

Chapter 11: When Our Hearts Get in the Way

1. Loren Eiseley, "The Star Thrower," in *The Unexpected Universe* (Orlando, FL: Harcourt Brace, 1969), 67–92.

2. Steve Corbett and Brian Fikkert, *When Helping Hurts: How to Alleviate Poverty Without Hurting the Poor . . . and Yourself* (Chicago: Moody, 2009).

3. Greg Nettle and Santiago "Jimmy" Mellado, *Small Matters: How Churches and Parents Can Raise Up World-Changing Children* (Grand Rapids: Zondervan, 2016), 23–24.

4. Søren Kierkegaard, *Provocations: Spiritual Writings of Kierkegaard* (Walden, NY: Plough, 2014), 193.

5. Timothy Keller, *The Freedom of Self-Forgetfulness: The Path to True Christian Joy* (Chorley, UK: 10Publishing, 2012), loc. 274, Kindle.
6. Bob Goff, *Everybody Always: Becoming Love in a World Full of Setbacks and Difficult People* (Nashville: Nelson Books, 2018), 205.

Chapter 12: When Little Children Get in the Way

1. J. P. Louw and E. A. Nida, *Greek-English Lexicon of the New Testament: Based on Semantic Domains*, 2nd ed. (New York: United Bible Societies, 1988), 1:760.
2. Aristides, "Apology 15," in *The Ante-Nicene Fathers*, ed. Allan Menzies, 5th ed. (New York: Scribner, 1926), 9:263–79.
3. John Ortberg, *Who Is This Man? The Unpredictable Impact of the Inescapable Jesus* (Grand Rapids: Zondervan, 2012), 25.
4. Charles Dickens, *A Christmas Carol* (New York: Bantam, Classics, 1986), 78.
5. Neil Gaiman, *Coraline* (New York: HarperCollins, 2002), ix. The G. K. Chesterton quote is from *Tremendous Trifles* (London: Forgotten Books, 2017), 130: "Fairy tales do not give the child his first idea of bogey. What fairy tales give the child is his first clear idea of the possible defeat of bogey. The baby has known the dragon intimately ever since he had an imagination. What the fairy tale provides for him is a St. George to kill the dragon."
6. The following story is taken from Rick Reilly, "Gainesville State High School Football Gets the Best Gift of All: Hope," ESPN.com, May 12, 2014, http://www.espn.com/espn/rickreilly/news/story?id=3789373.

Chapter 13: When Joyless, Selfish People Get in the Way

1. Used with permission.
2. Bob George, *Classic Christianity: Life's Too Short to Miss the Real Thing* (Eugene, OR: Harvest House, 1989), 134.

Chapter 14: When Christians Get in the Way

1. Mortimer Adler, quoted in Paul E. Little, *Know Why You Believe* (Downers Grove, IL: InterVarsity, 2000), 22.
2. Francis Collins, *The Language of God: A Scientist Presents Evidence for Belief* (New York: Free Press, 2006), 4.
3. From *Monty Python and The Holy Grail*, dir. Terry Gilliam and Terry Jones, EMI Films, 1975.
4. Collins, *Language of God*, 59.
5. Collins, *Language of God*, 3.

Conclusion: When Guilt Gets in the Way

1. C. S. Lewis, *Mere Christianity* (1952; repr., New York: HarperCollins, 2001), 69.
2. Dallas Willard, *The Divine Conspiracy* (San Francisco: HarperSanFrancisco, 1998), 329.

ABOUT THE AUTHOR

TIM HARLOW is the author of *Life on Mission* and senior pastor of Parkview Christian Church, one of the largest, fastest-growing churches in America. He has spent thirty years working with people who have baggage from their past church experiences. He knows what drives people away and that the Jesus of the Bible is ultimately the hope who brings them back. Tim and his wife make their home in the southern suburb of Chicago.